PRAISE FOR FREELANCE TO [...]

"I've come across a ton of information about fre[...] ...ncent has put together one of the top resources around, by j[...] ...reedom is honest, real, and exactly what a person needs to light the fi[...] ...r themselves to finally make a change in their life for the better."

Pat Flynn
Bestselling Author of Will It Fly, SmartPassiveIncome.com

"Interviewing over 1700 successful entrepreneurs has led me to one conclusion. Freedom is what we all crave. Freelance to Freedom *will be your guide to taking control of your time, your money and most importantly- your freedom."*

John Lee Dumas
Entrepreneur on Fire

*"*Freelance to Freedom *is full of inspirational and practical advice for anyone who wants to achieve financial freedom and live the American Dream. It's packed with real life examples and how-to's that will make a difference for those who apply it."*

Brian Moran
CEO & Founder, 12 Week Year

"Straight to the point and super timely. This book should be required reading to graduate high school as it can save millions from pursuing the American Dream that ends up being a nightmare."

John Ruhlin
Best Selling Author of Giftology

"Bracingly honest, direct and powerful—here are useful lessons from the trenches."

Seth Godin
Author, Linchpin

"The majority of people are sleepwalking through life, simply existing in their day jobs. Vincent reveals another way and another world. You can experience more freedom, finances, and fulfillment. This book is your guide to show you how."

Kary Oberbrunner
Author, Day Job to Dream Job

*"*Freelance To Freedom *is the roadmap to define and realize financial and life success. It is a must read for everyone who wants to be in the drivers seat of their own future."*

Deb Ingino
CEO StrengthLeader.com

"Financial freedom is not a mythical beast that our modern society makes it out to be. It's simple, attainable, and you can start right now where you are. Freelance to Freedom *will show you how."*

Shawn Stevenson
Bestselling Author of Sleep Smarter, The Model Health Show

"A great reminder that we're all standing on our own "acres of diamonds." We create our opportunities - they are not thrust upon us. Read this as a new set of eyes to discover the wealth right in front of you."

Dan Miller
Author and coach, 48 Days

FREELANCE TO FREEDOM

FREELANCE
TO
FREEDOM

The Roadmap for Creating a Side
Business to Achieve Financial,
Time and Life Freedom

VINCENT PUGLIESE

NEW YORK

LONDON • NASHVILLE • MELBOURNE • VANCOUVER

FREELANCE TO FREEDOM

The Roadmap for Creating a Side Business to Achieve
Financial, Time and Life Freedom

© 2018 Vincent Pugliese

Published in New York, New York, by Morgan James Publishing. Morgan James is a
trademark of Morgan James, LLC. www.MorganJamesPublishing.com

The Morgan James Speakers Group can bring authors to your live event. For more
information or to book an event visit The Morgan James Speakers Group at
www.TheMorganJamesSpeakersGroup.com.

ISBN 9781683504566 - paperback
ISBN 9781683504573 - eBook
Library of Congress Control Number: 2017902205

Cover Design by: Vincent Pugliese and Chris Trccani
3dogcreative.net

Interior Design by: Paul Curtis

In an effort to support local communities, raise awareness and funds, Morgan James
Publishing donates a percentage of all book sales for the life of each book to
Habitat for Humanity Peninsula and Greater Williamsburg.

Get involved today! Visit
www.MorganJamesBuilds.com

DEDICATION

To my incredible, supportive and loving wife, Elizabeth, and our three creative, thoughtful and amazing sons, Andrew, Nolan and Dylan - You are the four people in this world that I want to make the most proud.

TABLE OF CONTENTS

INTRODUCTION

The secret of happiness is freedom. The secret of freedom is courage.
—Thucydides

I n 2008, my wife Elizabeth and I gained our financial freedom. More importantly, as a result of that, we gained our time freedom. With that freedom comes the ability to shape and craft each day as we decide. Now, we have an extraordinary amount of time to spend with our family. We both do work that we love, and we have money to do it.

Looking around, that actually makes us exceedingly rare. How we got here isn't something I've spoken of often. Talking money isn't a fun topic for most adults, particularly when one or more participants in the conversation isn't doing well with their time or money. But when the conversation comes up, the same question is always asked:

"How did you do it?"

Each friend who asks that question—usually in private—has the same things in common. They are overworked at a job they don't enjoy, stressed on time and in so much debt that it appears as though it is now a part of them like an extra

3

body part. They have a dream to be self-employed, but they already don't get enough time with their children to even dream of starting something on the side. Their marriages are stressed, and they feel completely overwhelmed.

Elizabeth and I never struck it rich with the lottery. There wasn't an inheritance. We started on our journey more than $140,000 in debt, with a child on the way, while earning $15 per hour. When we escaped that crushing debt and low-paying jobs, I realized that not only should I write this, I have an obligation to do so.

People are looking for inspiration and are in desperate need of positive vibes in this era of negative and depressing news. I am thrilled to share the great news I have for you. For a long time, I wondered what I could add to the conversation about financial and time freedom, until my friend David Burke said something that changed my mindset.

"Your story inspires me. Dude, this is the story about how you did it. That is why it's different. I've never heard the behind-the-scenes story of how someone actually did it."

Not only is it possible to become financially free while being self-employed, it's easier than you think. Oh, it's hard to do, don't get me wrong, but it's easier than you think. It's completely doable to have the time you crave with your family, do the work you actually love to do, and have the money to do it.

What's This About?

This is not a book about money. It's not about stocks or investing. There aren't any charts, formulas, or bar graphs. It isn't even necessarily about trying to make *more* money.

This is about freedom. It's about creating time. It's about living a life where you aren't stuck in a job you hate. It's about creating a life doing what you want to do instead of working daily to pay for things you already bought. It's about rejecting the popular notion that doing what is normal is going to get you anywhere besides where you already are.

Of course, money has a lot to do with that. The late, great Zig Ziglar said that "Money isn't the most important thing in life, but it's up there with oxygen on the 'gotta have it' scale." But our culture of consumerism and debt has stifled our progress. It has strangled our creativity. It has pushed our college students, lugging five- and six-figure student loans, into jobs they took only to pay for those student loans—which, for some, will take most of their adult lives. It has created a nation where people no longer wonder if you have a car payment, but how much it is and for how long.

What makes me qualified to write this book? Nothing and everything.

I don't have a finance degree. I'm not a "money expert". But my wife and I have lived a debt-free life while being self-employed, and we've been able to shape the life for our family we used to dream about. As I write this, a new year is about to begin and our budget for the entire year is set and accounted for. I get to wake up every day and choose what I will work on. That's the thing about freedom. You choose your life instead of someone else choosing it for you.

I'm not saying this to brag. I'm saying this to let you know that a life of financial, time, and life freedom is possible. And if we can do it, you can, too.

What is this book about? Part I of the book is the story of our journey, with no embarrassing details left out. At 32, I was completely stuck, deep in debt, in a low paying job with a baby on the way. In less than four years, my wife Elizabeth and I were totally debt free, house included. We quit our jobs, became financially and time free and did the work we loved. All because of taking an underutilized skill and turning it into a side business.

Part I was how we did it. Part II is how you can do it. And trust me, you can do it. Here is a brief breakdown of the five phases, which we will go through in Part II.

Phase I — Escaping the Seeds of Discontent

Phase I, unfortunately, is where a majority of the workforce finds itself. Eighty percent of employees do not like their jobs. They are looking for a way out, but feel stuck. They often have little money saved, are stretched for time, have fallen into an unhealthy lifestyle, and have stress in their home lives.

At the same time, most do have a dream to do something different. Commonly, it is not to find a different full-time job. Instead, they feel drawn to starting a side business doing something they have a passion for. They have a desire to help others in some way. They want better control of their time. They want opportunity to make more money. And they want more time with their kids and their spouse. But they feel stuck, lost, and unsure where to start.

Phase II — The Side Hustle

This is a phase of tremendous growth. It also comes with a lot of pain. If you didn't have a side business already, this is where you start one. It's also where you see so many of the mistakes that you made in the past. You learn the difference between being an entrepreneur and a freelancer, figure out what you actually love doing, and go through tremendous growing pains.

It's where you start to get control of the money you have, shape a plan for the future, and get a glimpse of the life you truly desire. This is the phase where you make your biggest business mistakes and learn your greatest lessons, setting you up for the growth you will see in Phase III.

Phase III — The Optimal Freelancer

In Phase III, things are looking up.

You are bringing in more than 50% of the income you need to live off from your business. You may have already quit your day job, or are close to doing so. You are now paying down your debt with your business income. You've researched all your investment options and have the insurance you need to protect you from danger.

Your family life is also in a better place. You are more attentive to your family. The stress and drama you felt is beginning to fade. You are more energized than anxious. You realize that with money freedom comes mental freedom. With more mental freedom, you start coming up with new ideas, which is when you have the ability to easily shift between freelancer to entrepreneur. This is the stage when your business, time, and money start to fire at an optimal level.

Phase IV — A Life of Freedom

What would it be like to wake up every day and do exactly what you want to do? What would it feel like to not owe anyone else a dime? What would it feel like to have the abundant time to devote to your spouse, children, and friends?

On top of that, you have a healthy lifestyle, free to exercise without trying to find the time and to eat well without trying to find the money. Phase IV is when an unexpected setback is like driving over a pebble when it used to be like driving into a ditch. You don't have to work as much, but you do because you want to grow, help others, and contribute. It makes you feel alive. You can't see the difference between working and playing.

The clients you take on are hand-selected, and you have the financial freedom to turn down the clients who aren't a good fit. With this extra time and money, it's easy to create time for ideas that can bring in passive income, sending you deeper into Phase IV. It's the area where nearly every self-employed person dreams of being, but where very few get.

Phase V — Every Day Is Independence Day

Phase V is simple. Time freedom. Financial freedom. Location freedom. Life freedom. What more could you want?

Why Am I Writing This?

This topic means so much to me because, as a teenager, money problems almost destroyed my family.

My parents work life provided me with a preview of what my future might look like. My mom held a steady government job for thirty years, going part-time while my brother and I were young. My dad always had an entrepreneurial spirit.

My mom saw the advantages and the benefits provided from a secure job. My dad grew up starting small businesses throughout his childhood, from selling lemonade to newspaper routes, and dry-cleaning pickups, and carried that into adulthood.

Both methods worked well, but I leaned tremendously toward self-employment. From a young age, I watched my dad run a business from our basement as a freelance draftsman in the construction industry. He moved on to become a salesman for a construction products company, and then worked as an estimator. That position turned into a partnership for a new business, which was successful from the start. That was until the bottom dropped out overnight.

I was a normal fifteen-year-old kid when I woke up one morning to find my father face down on the living-room couch. I didn't think much of it, except that when I came home, he was still on the couch.

The previous night, the world my parents knew shattered with one phone call. His partner had emptied $135,000 from their bank account and moved to a different state with his wife and family. Business checks bounced, as none of the bills could be paid. My father was held liable for all the contracts, and there were liens placed on our home for more than one million dollars. In one swift, shocking, and immoral move, my dad's business was on life support.

With no money for the business, the construction jobs they were working on stopped immediately. My dad, in utter shock, found solace curled up on the couch. My mom needed to go to work, and my brother and I would walk past him to school. The shock turned to panic as calls started coming in questioning the unfinished job sites. There were hazardous materials on site, and he was now responsible for removing them—without the money to do so.

This nightmare continued for months. Our home life consisted of phone calls about lawsuits, tension, fights, and arguments between each of us in the house. The low point came when a television news report named my dad in a story they did on the jobs his business had not completed. Money got so tight that I overheard my parents talking about finding another place to live.

I mentally—and often physically—checked out of school. One afternoon, while cutting science class again, I sat alone and dejected along the window facing the school courtyard inside Roslyn High School. The principal, Mr. Diden, noticed two things. One, I should be in class. Two, and more valuable to me, was the pain on my face. He put his arm on my shoulder and didn't ask where I should be. He asked what was wrong.

I told him my parents were having severe money problems, and I had no idea what was going to happen.

He asked me to go to his office, where we talked about it all. I told him about what happened to my dad's business. I broke down about the daily money issues my mom and dad were dealing with. I explained the incredible amount of tension in our house, and how I felt like I didn't belong there anymore. I had already run away twice to sleep in the park, only to realize that I was powerless on my own.

On the rare occasions that my dad and I did talk, it was in the form of a disagreement. I hated all of it and wanted to be anywhere but there. Filled with anger, confusion and sadness, everything looked depressingly hopeless.

Amid the turmoil, I walked downstairs to go to work when my dad stopped me at the bottom of the stairs. In what had to be nothing short of demoralizing, he paused before asking if he could borrow $700. All I could think about on my way to work was how hard it must have been for my father to ask his fifteen-year-old son for a loan.

But after months of crippling depression, my dad got off the couch. His mood improved, his confidence returned, and he got back in the game. He began a new rebar detailing business, and the contacts and relationships that he built while freelancing years back helped it grow fast enough that my parents kept up with the lien payments and held onto the house. Although their money situation improved, the relationship between my dad and I didn't. Their financial disaster, and the effects from it, took a tremendous toll on our relationship. It would be another decade before we enjoyed being around each other again.

Six Years of Failure

Six years later, this whole "life thing" wasn't working out for me.

I barely graduated high school, learning on the last day of final exams that I just slid by. I was arrogant, stubborn, and defiant. Majoring in five different subjects in college, I dropped out of each of them. This wasn't Yale. This was Nassau Community College. I was accepted because I breathed air.

My parents, conversely, turned their entire situation around. They worked together, scraping and clawing, and got back on track. Not only did they pay off all those business loans, expenses, and fines, they managed to pay off their home mortgage, as well, in less than seven years.

I didn't follow their example. Going through a dozen low-end jobs, I turned into a thief, to the point of being arrested and handcuffed in front of my co-workers for stealing cassette tapes from the music store factory where I worked. I didn't learn the lesson, continuing my illegal ways by stealing from my next job, too. I wasn't caught that time, but I woke up in the middle of the night in a cold sweat after a nightmare about being caught again. I went downstairs, distraught and frightened, sitting alone in the kitchen. I asked myself one question.

"What Am I Doing With My Life?"

I kept asking myself that question over and over. I realized it was impossible to run away from my discontent any longer. This was my reality. All at once, it hit me that I had never taken my life seriously. Back to my elementary school days, through high school, random community college classes, and my indiscriminate gaggle of jobs, I was the poster boy for a twenty-two-year-old slacker.

So, I sat at that circular wooden table alone. Alone, and full of regrets. These weren't regrets of failure. They were regrets of never trying. I angrily admitted that I cared more about sports and music than my own life. I remembered what my friend Ben asked after I got upset watching my favorite team, the Pittsburgh Steelers, lose a game. "Why do you care so much? When these athletes are driving home to their mansions," he asked, "do you think they're upset about how you did at work today?"

I was puzzled why I cared more about their lives than my own.

Not long after, my father broke the silence by coming downstairs for a glass of water. My dad and I still had a rough relationship. We had butted heads for as long as I could remember, and I felt like he never understood me. I was starting to see why. I didn't understand me.

He noticed a problem and asked what was bothering me. I raised my voice, finally angry at myself instead of everyone else.

"I have no idea what I'm doing with my life."

He looked at me, looked away, and then right back at me. He gave a quick, to-the-point response. "You enjoy taking pictures. You like sports. You like traveling. Why don't you go take a photography class? Maybe you could be a photographer."

He gave me a look of wisdom, patted my shoulder, and went back to bed. I slowly felt the blood in my body revive as I lifted my head.

"Photography?" I said out loud. I knew nothing about it. I didn't know the first place to start. It was frightening, but in a good way. I sat back in the chair and allowed myself to envision the dream scenario. Instead of being a lump on the couch watching sports on television, I pictured myself on the sidelines photographing games for a living.

"I have to try this," I said to myself with a conviction I had never felt before. I also figured this would probably fail because I failed at everything in my life, but at least I'd fail doing something cool.

The next morning, I was at a camera store making an emotional, uneducated, and expensive purchase of an SLR camera. I jumped right in, afraid that I would back out if I didn't make a commitment. I signed up for photography classes at Nassau Community College the next day. My sixth major.

I Have to Make It

"Twenty years from now you will be more disappointed by the things that you didn't do than by the ones you did do." —**Mark Twain**

Even though I was only twenty-two, I was at a crossroads.

If I went into this half-hearted like I did with everything else, my future was clear—and it wasn't pretty. There were enough middle-aged men working in the two dead end jobs that I had to see things don't just magically get better. There was a pattern among these men: quiet, sarcastic, bitter, and generally negative about life. It was crystal clear that they never expected this to be the life they wound up with.

With a wife, kids, and a mortgage, they meekly accepted this life they unwittingly chose. These men would show up at work each day, often the slight aroma of alcohol still on their breath from the night before. They worked a job that paid the bills by day, then drowned their sorrows in a bottle by night. Repeat this pattern night after night, year after year.

All my years of not caring finally caught up with me. Time, it turns out, really does not slow down. I have to make this happen. I HAVE to. This felt like my last chance.

If I didn't give this photography thing everything I had, I was going to be a forty-five-year-old alcoholic, overweight, and divorced, with kids I never saw, who didn't even like me. I was going to live paycheck to paycheck, and was going to be angry. Every morning I pictured this future me. It made my heart race. It made my blood boil. It made me so frightened that I punched the steering wheel with tears in my eyes as I drove back to that job.

For once in your life, I told myself, *give something everything you've got. Is that too much to ask?*

The Bottom Rung

Every night, I studied my camera and the photographs in the newspaper. Five nights a week, I bought the cheapest ticket to a baseball or football game, camera on my shoulder, and finagled my way close to the field to try to take a decent picture. I finally got the courage to start asking the professional photographers shooting the game for advice on how to take better pictures.

After calling more than 100 newspapers and magazines to obtain an internship or an entry level job—and being rejected by each one—I finally got my first break.

It was a nice gig, although unpaid. It was for Bruce Bennett Studios, a company that shot professional hockey games, and to my good fortune, turned out to be the team photographers for my favorite hockey team, the New York Rangers. I wasn't a photographer—more like a gopher. When I wasn't working there for free, I was a restaurant waiter and a technician at a camera store. But after nine months of nagging, I finally got to shoot my first game—Rangers vs. Penguins—at Madison Square Garden in New York City, two days before my twenty-fourth birthday.

More than a year into the gig, I elevated to minimum wage. I even had a new nickname at work: Vinimum Wage. That was an upgrade from my previous nickname, The Vintern. My foot was barely in the door, but it was in. And unlike all my other failed attempts, I was not going to let this door close.

Within a year, I got my first internship at *Newsday*, a major New York newspaper with the sixth largest readership in the country at the time. Soon after I would be published in various publications throughout the country while freelancing for different news and sports publications. I took on gigs that included traveling to shoot for the World Wrestling Federation, The National Hockey League, the National Football League, and The Associated Press.

I still didn't make much money, but the dream was taking shape.

Soon after, I was accepted to The School of Visual Communications at Ohio University, one of the top photojournalism programs in the country. This time, I was ready to dominate school as opposed to it dominating me. I only had two years left to graduate, so I had to make things happen quickly. With the sense of urgency only a twenty-six-year-old in classes with eighteen-year-olds can muster, I put the pedal to the metal. No excuses, no slacking, and no wasting time.

Aside from spending time with an adorable girl named Elizabeth I met during my second semester, I dug in.

For the first time in my academic life, I was held up in class as an example and not a warning. Near the end of my time in Ohio, I was selected as a finalist in the William Randolph Hearst National Championship, arguably the highest award for college photojournalism in the nation. During a multiple-day competition in San Francisco, competing against five of the top shooters in the country, I was selected Grand Champion for the competition. I returned to Ohio with $6,000 in prize money, much-needed validation, and most importantly, momentum.

You see, that momentum parlayed into my first steady, paying photography job. After a year of searching, offers finally started coming in. It seems one little award can go a long way sometimes, because it led to jobs at the same newspaper for Elizabeth and me. Right after graduation, Elizabeth and I headed to Evansville, Indiana, to start our careers as staff photographers at the *Courier & Press*.

PART I

FOUR YEARS TO FREEDOM

Becoming Normal

We settled in nicely in Evansville. It's a challenging adjustment for a New Yorker to adapt to the Midwestern lifestyle, but it was working. The job was good, although I was never comfortable as an employee. My assignments consisted of spot news, various news stories, features, local sports and portraits. I missed shooting professional sports, so on my own time, I would obtain credentials through the newspaper and travel to St. Louis, Nashville, Cincinnati, and Indianapolis to shoot the Rams, Cardinals, Colts, Titans, Bengals, and Reds games to get my fix.

A year later, Elizabeth and I were engaged. Our salaries combined were just above $60,000, so we needed to be cautious about how our wedding would affect our money situation. Aside from the credit cards we used, and $12,000 in student loans, we didn't have much debt, and we didn't want to go in deeper for the wedding.

Sitting at the kitchen table to crunch the numbers, we devised a plan. The wedding was a year away. If we could each save $400 a week from our checks, we would be able to pay for the entire thing in cash. Diligent and focused, we nailed the wedding budget like a finely tuned machine.

As the big day approached, our apartment lease was ending and we wanted out. Neither of us had any desire to start our married life together living above the crazy couple who fought every night and the angry lady living to our right. It was time to go house shopping.

Clueless about how to purchase a house, we drove around the east side of Evansville every evening to see what was out there. New Yorkers are raised listening to stories about how expensive houses are. I was excited to see that homes in this Midwestern town were a fraction of what my friends were paying back home.

We found a cute house with ugly brown and green paint and fell in love with it. It was "For Sale by Owner", so we cautiously knocked on the front door. Kirk and Christy, the young parents of two boys, invited us in and gave us the tour. Elizabeth and I were hooked immediately. Our negotiating skills were void as we managed to only drop the price by $1,000, but at least we got them to add in the refrigerator. (You don't want us handling your next contract negotiation.) The final price was $126,900, and just like that, we were in!

Debt People

The week our bid was accepted, my black Chevy Beretta was struggling through its final days. I only had a car payment once before, and I hated it. But with all our money tied up in the wedding and the down payment for the house, I loosened up a bit and bought an $11,000 Saturn a few weeks before our wedding. Mortgage? Check. Car payment? Check. Student loans? Check. We were on our way to being normal, and normal is not a good thing.

Elizabeth and I returned from our sun-drenched honeymoon in Saint Lucia to our new life, our new house, and my new car. I sat in my metallic-blue car on my way to work and instead of enjoying the new(er) car smell, I felt uneasy that we now owed a bunch of money. But that's normal, right?

Everyone tells you debt is normal. I realized I didn't know anyone who didn't have debt. My grandfather used to say that you can count on two things in life: death and taxes. I guess it's actually three things: death, taxes, and debt.

My uneasiness went away quickly, because when you have a new house, you need stuff to go in it. We brought our old futon and creaky bed with us. We made do with the junky kitchen table from our apartment. But we also financed our couch set for our living room.

Debt is like tattoos: once you have one, it's really easy to add more. That's why I was never comfortable getting that first tattoo. Next thing I know, I'd be washing my face in the morning to see it covered with ink like Mike Tyson.

Looking Good and Feeling Bad

The debt made us look good, though! Our house was coming together nicely. The sun flowed in magnificently through the double doors in our living room, brightening up the entire floor. We painted and mowed the lawn like any good citizen. We even got the dog! Lola, our fluffy, cuddly Golden Retriever, was the first addition to our family eight months after our wedding.

The first big purchase we made on credit was the big screen television I talked Elizabeth into. This was all me. She didn't watch it often, but I convinced her that we needed a high-definition, 50-inch television dominating our family room. In 2003, it was a showstopper. It was also expensive. We took out a store credit card for the entire balance of $2,500. It was one of those no-interest cards—as long as the balance was paid by a certain date.

The debt slowly tightened its grip on us. Between a mortgage, car payment, television, student loan, and furniture, we were no longer as comfortable as we were before the wedding. It obviously wasn't affecting me much because that's when I decided we needed a complete overhaul of our damp basement.

I talked Elizabeth into the major project. I would bust down the existing walls, rip out the cruddy steps, and replace them both with beautiful new ones. I would put in a ceramic tile floor throughout, complete with a radiant heat system underneath the tiles. On the right side of the room would be a pool table with hanging blue lights. On the left would be a custom-built bar we would create ourselves.

And we would pay for it all with plastic.

Dave Who?

From the moment I put the hammer through drywall, we were neck deep in a huge project. Day after day, hour after hour, all my time away from work was spent remodeling the basement. Never mind that up until this point, the extent of my "handiness" was limited to painting our kitchen.

When I wasn't in the basement, I was at work. That summer, I was marked down for a number of photo assignments in Southern Illinois, a rural area the newspaper was making a push into to grow readership. I drew the short straw to cover the quiet little towns dotting the lower part of the state. The drives, which could vary between an hour and two hours, challenged my sanity. Once the Evansville radio stations were out of range, I had access to the wide variety of three different country music stations. This was pre-smartphone, and the CD player in my car didn't work.

It was on one of these humdrum drives when I heard the twangy voice of some hillbilly-sounding man taking calls about money. I initially took him as some local radio guy for whom I'd just doubled his audience by tuning in. But the next caller was from San Antonio, Texas. A few minutes later, someone from Denver, Colorado, called in. As I cruised through the backroads of towns like Carmi and Eldorado, I found myself trying hard to hang onto his words as the radio reception got worse. His voice faded away into the dusty roads. This was information I needed to hear. *I didn't even get your name*, I thought, like some jilted dude at a bar as that girl walked away.

Two days later, I was sent to photograph the practice of the Harrisburg football team. Scanning through my limited options again, this guy's voice jumped out of my speakers. He was railing on some guy about his car payment. I nodded righteously in agreement. *Who takes out a car payment like that?* I thought while driving in my car that had a payment on it. He tackled all sorts of money issues.

He even related them to how money affects relationships. It was all so freaking interesting. And I wondered to myself, *Have I become this lame? Instead of listening to music or sports talk, I'm listening to a money show and loving it.* But I still didn't know who this guy was.

Finally, before throwing to break, he declared, *"You are listening to The Dave Ramsey Show."*

Hmmmm, never heard of him. I drove back to the newspaper to see if anyone had heard of this guy. Was he from around here? Nothing. Nobody knew who he was. I was as curious as I was confused. This stuff was too good to be hidden on some backwoods radio station. I searched the local stations to see if he was on anywhere in Evansville, but he wasn't.

The very next day, instead of dreading the Illinois assignment, I volunteered for it. I apparently needed my daily fix.

For a few months, I looked forward to any opportunity to listen to his show. I would take notes at the end of my drive about his methods. He practiced a thing called "baby steps," which was a seven-step formula for getting out of debt and becoming financially free. So, as I continued to pile up debt daily with the black hole basement renovation, I nodded arrogantly in agreement as Dave educated debt-ridden callers on their financial mistakes.

Heading Toward the Cellar

By September, the cashiers at Home Depot knew me by name. I made a purchase there at least once a day for the past month. With a goal of having the basement completed for our big New Year's Eve party, I justified the spending as a temporary thing. I justified the debt as normal—like almost all the callers told Ramsey before he tried to set them straight.

Thousands of dollars of new debt later, we were entering the home stretch. December arrived, and we were weeks away from our self-imposed deadline. The radiant heat was now flowing through the floors of our basement, warming the room from the bottom with a simple twist of the thermostat. The tile was installed and grouted. The walls were up and painted. The pool table was ordered and on its way.

The final piece of the puzzle was the bar. We had designed it in an L shape, and the thick polyurethane top had settled and begun drying. Elizabeth took on the project of doing a mosaic tile design that would encompass the entire lower level of the bar. We were tired, but pushed on. Our credit card was just as exhausted from all the swipes it took at the home-improvement stores and our holiday shopping. It was then, in mid-December, that Elizabeth and I took a vacation to Colorado. It was a relaxing few days at a ski resort that I remember as much for the newspaper headline of the capture of Saddam Hussein as the beautiful Rocky Mountains.

At the Denver airport, I strolled into a bookstore where I came upon *The Total Money Makeover*, Dave Ramsey's book that I heard him plug on-air. I had slipped from listening to the show when my assignments in Illinois dwindled. I had lost my "gazelle intensity," as Dave would say. As Elizabeth waited by our gate, I plucked down my credit card to purchase a book about getting out of debt. Irony personified.

I had heard the man, but I had failed to listen. I spent months agreeing with his money advice while we dug ourselves deeper into debt. It was to the point that I didn't even want to look at our statements. We were heading down an unsustainable path, and the tension from it was affecting my sleep. On the flight home, Elizabeth slept on my shoulder as I studied the book like I was preparing for a final exam. It was an easy read, to be honest. I mean, it was all common sense. I knew all of this—I just didn't do any of it. It seemed easy to do. But doing the easy thing is also so hard, because if it's easy to do, it's also easy not to do.

Having all the baby steps written out gave me clarity. In the book, Dave has a page where you write out all your debts. As painful as it was, I poured out our mistakes with ink inside his book. When I saw the numbers, my heart sank as if the airplane hit a patch of intense turbulence. Between the house, student loans, my car, furniture, the home-improvement store cards, and our credit cards, we had accumulated more than $140,000 of debt in just eighteen months.

For two people talking about starting a family, we were being as stupid as possible. Somewhere above St. Louis I realized we were doing everything wrong. Elizabeth awoke to a husband who had a different sort of awakening. She laughed when she saw my eyes. At first she thought something was wrong, until she understood I was now in "intense psycho" mode.

"We need to get out of debt," I urged her. As I whispered louder than she wanted me to, she looked at me as if I were trying to enter a cult. I tried to let her know that this was a good thing, and I wasn't going off the deep end. We returned home to prepare for our New Year's bash and the unveiling of "Pugliese's Tavern". My parents and brother, along with Elizabeth's mom, were traveling in for the celebration, along with forty or so friends that would ring in the New Year with us.

We had no money, but the finishing touches for the basement needed to be completed. By the afternoon of New Year's Eve, I had already read The Total Money Makeover twice. I wasn't able to convince Elizabeth to pay down the debt, but I was able to persuade her to agree to not use credit cards anymore. We needed to start somewhere. My brother Steve joined me on one final Home Depot run for the last few light bulbs and screws we needed to finish the basement. I swiped my credit card and told him that I would never use a credit card again.

We were done. Even though we technically hadn't done anything, for the first time in a long while it felt like we were going in the right direction. I had a slight sense of peace as we prepared for the party. If we stopped using the cards, we would never be in any more debt than we were at that moment.

The New Year's Eve party was an enormous success. We partied deep into the night and rang in the New Year, and for us, a new life, with a house filled with friends, family, and love.

January 1st arrived with a hangover and a mission. We weren't getting out of debt starting this year. We were getting out of debt starting right now. This was not a resolution. This was not a goal. This was a life change. Well, at least as far as I was concerned. Elizabeth still thought I was losing my mind. And she wasn't the only one.

Becoming Weird

I was talking about our plan with a co-worker when another photographer overheard our conversation. He was in his mid-50's and listened intently as I laid it out. He snickered like I was an 11-year-old telling him I was going to play professional baseball when I grow up.

He finally cut in when I told him we had just cut up our credit cards. "What? That's insane," he lectured me. "How will you pay for things?"

"With cash," I answered.

He looked at me like I was growing a second head. The idea of paying cash was now such a foreign thought. I understood then that we were going to be the weird ones.

The first goal was to save $1,000 in a "baby emergency fund". The idea is to have something put away just in case something unexpected comes up as you begin paying down debt. The enthusiasm I spoke with around my co-workers faded when I realized our debt and expenses accounted for all the income we brought in from our jobs. It's a dreary outlook when the idea of saving $1,000 is a struggle. And even if we could, I was conflicted. Shouldn't we just start paying down the debt we had and worry about the emergency fund later? And what about our retirement or investing? At thirty-three years old, I had barely saved anything. As much as I loved the idea of the baby steps, it felt overwhelming.

At this point, I had found Ramsey's radio show on a station in town. The job of a photojournalist means spending more time in the car than it does shooting photographs, so I took advantage of that every afternoon. Listening to caller after caller experiencing almost exactly what we were going through gave Elizabeth and me the first push we needed. One gentleman wouldn't give up going out to eat to get the emergency fund going for his family. Dave asked how that was working for him. It was then that I knew our behaviors and habits, even today, were contributing to our malaise.

I checked our bank statements to see that we spent enough money eating out and at Target the previous month to fund the first baby step! That was a hard conversation to bring up with my lovely wife. We were both financially out of shape, but unlike Elizabeth, who had begun training to run her first half marathon, I was on my way to being physically out of shape, as well.

Tightening the belt hurts literally and figuratively when you are in debt and overweight. The start is the hardest part when you are not used to sacrificing. Our first sacrifice came from a reduction in eating out. We had a serious sit-down about where our money was actually going. Just like most of our friends thought, we also didn't believe we had a dime to spare. But by early February, we had cut our restaurant trips in half, got tough on Target, and finally had $1,000 saved in a baby emergency fund. It was the smallest of goals, but the satisfaction of sacrificing gave us a jolt of positive financial momentum we hadn't had since getting married.

The Next Step

The next list of debts to tackle commenced in February. It was hard not to be discouraged looking at our list. It read like this: Lowe's, Home Depot, Value City Furniture, VISA credit card, my car, and a student loan. That didn't take into consideration our mortgage. As I dug in, Elizabeth casually went along.

"Whatever you want to do, honey," was her sweet response.

I realized early on she wasn't going to be into this like I was. I won't say she fought me on the quest to get out of debt, but we weren't on the same page either. I set the course with hope that she would see the light along the way.

The Lowe's credit card was the first one we attacked. It was followed by the Home Depot card. The power of momentum was in full force. I was so focused that I would have sold my car and walked to work if I didn't need it for assignments. By early May, we knocked off the Value City store card, as well as the remainder of our VISA card.

Do you remember the big screen television we bought? We eventually paid that in full. At least we thought we had. We made the payment of $2,500 eight months before any interest was due. After that date passed, we received a surprising letter stating that we owed the full amount of interest for the entire time of the loan.

There was more than seven hundred dollars' worth of interest owed. Trying to fight back a heart attack, I looked over their explanation. In the details, they described that we paid $2,500, but the balance was $2,500.09. They explained that because those nine cents weren't paid for—and for which we hadn't received a single bill in the eight months—we were on the hook for all the interest from the start.

I flipped out. Flipped out! I called the collection agency in full attack mode. I had all the paperwork and the details. I can't tell you how many people I spoke to. It had to be everyone in that filthy company. They finally admitted that they had made a mistake and relieved us from the interest payments. Never again, we said. Never again.

After that fiasco, all that stood in our way of completing Baby Step Two was my car payment, which was around $11,000, and the student loan, which was around $12,000.

The Changeover

It was on a drive to New York when everything changed. Through all of this, Elizabeth hadn't read *The Total Money Makeover*. I was upset by her lack of commitment because I was convinced that this was the best plan for us. I just needed her to be on board if we were going to really change our lives. We were now looking to start a family. Looking back on my teenage years, I desperately did not want to be struggling with money when we had kids.

During the two-day, fifteen-hour trek from Indiana to the Big Apple, Elizabeth agreed to read the book. To make sure she had no distractions while she read, I kept the radio off. I was so curious about her response that I kept watching her facial expressions out of the corner of my eye. I knew that if she was lukewarm toward the ideas, we were never going to be as free as I envisioned.

The moment of truth finally arrived. She closed the book, took a deep breath, and smiled at me.

"Let's get out of debt," she announced. "Let's do this!"

If you have ever seen the movie *Rocky II*, you might remember my favorite scene. Rocky was scheduled to fight Apollo Creed in a rematch for the Heavyweight Championship of the World. His wife, Adrian, was pregnant with their first baby and fell into a coma. Rocky was emotionally distraught and unable to train for this dangerous fight.

Day after day, he sat by her side or in the chapel praying. His trainer, Mickey, tried unsuccessfully to get Rocky to see the severity of not preparing for the fight.

Rocky held her hand in the hospital bed, and when Adrian's fingers began to move, his eyes widened as she came out of the coma. After their emotional embrace, Rocky tells Adrian that he will back out of the fight and find another way to make ends meet. She looks at him, and with a resolve that was palpable, says the words that change the course of Rocky's life and career.

"There's one thing I want you to do for me," she whispers to her husband. "Win."

Rocky slowly pulls his head back in disbelief. It was the last thing he expected to hear from his wife who had pleaded for him to stop fighting in fear for his health.

"Win," she said again in a more determined way.

"Whadda we waitin' for?" Mickey screams. And the rest is history, as Rocky went on to win the championship.

Now, I wasn't fighting for the world championship, and thankfully, Elizabeth wasn't coming out of a coma, but her words had the same effect on me that Adrian's had on Rocky. I looked out onto the bright Pennsylvania interstate and knew that we were on our way to an incredible life. There was nothing stopping us from becoming free.

What Does Freedom Mean?

Freedom means something different to everyone. At that moment in our lives, Elizabeth and I were both employed for a newspaper. That industry was about to be hit with a seismic change that would forever shift the landscape, like so many are feeling today. We were beginning to feel the rumblings. Being a sports photographer with the paper, the assignments and travel with the NFL was one of the reasons I put up with so much of the other minutiae that went with working at a daily newspaper.

But when the budget for travel and those assignments began to dry up, my passion for that job dwindled. At the same time, we were trying to start a family, and our unpredictable hours gave us both many nights with little sleep. Our hours changed every month from a 9:00 a.m. shift, to a 2:00 p.m. shift, to an 11:00 a.m. shift. In between were all types of schedule changes and breaking news which pulled at least one of us out of bed at night. No matter how we broke it down, there was no way we were both able to work there and have the life we wanted.

That's why it became extra important to get ourselves onto the same page. When Elizabeth finished that book and came on board, it was the assurance I needed to do what Adrian, and now Elizabeth said: "Win."

We returned from New York and worked the numbers together for the first time. We cut back and actually began to enjoy it. Less spending meant less stuff. Less stuff meant less clutter. Elizabeth agreed that it wasn't as painful as she had thought. We did our budget together and actively started looking for extra freelance photography assignments to throw directly at the car and student loans. Assignments we didn't even know existed suddenly became available to us. It's amazing what happens once you open your eyes.

Elizabeth and I got to experience that sense of pride together. It was no longer a constraint. It seemed like every dollar not meant for food, bills, or the mortgage went straight to reducing debt. That can't be far from the truth because our take-home pay from our full-time jobs was somewhere around $45,000 a year.

Real Baby Steps Are Coming

We then received the amazing news that Elizabeth was pregnant with our first child!

The timing of it all seemed surreal. No, we weren't where we wanted to be. Not by a long shot. There was no retirement savings and only a minimal emergency fund, but we now had a little bambino to support. And we still had a car payment, student loan, and a mortgage to take care of. Still, we had gotten rid of enough financial gnats that had been flying around our heads that we were able to breathe better.

As we focused on the pregnancy, we took a break from our intense money goals of the past year. I slowed down searching for freelance work, and Elizabeth tried to catch up on her sleep. I had no idea how tired creating a baby can make a girl. New Year's Eve was 180 degrees different than the year before. Instead of rocking out until 4:00 a.m., we were sleeping on the couch hours before the ball dropped.

As any expectant dad can attest to, the thought of having a child changes you in ways you would never understand until you actually go through it. I doled out all sorts of comments, opinions, and advice to friends with kids over the years. I was arrogant enough to think that because I took care of my nieces and nephews for hours at a time, I had any clue what I was talking about.

I remember telling my co-worker, Tom Lovett, who was discussing an issue regarding his three-year-old, to "reason" with him. The other dads in the room laughed hard when I administered my sage advice.

"Reason with him?" he replied jokingly.

I stood firm in my stance. As they continued their conversation no longer looking for my input, I remember thinking I was spot on. We've had a three-year-old three times and I can say, without a shadow of a doubt, that I was a moron when I said that.

The euphoria of becoming parents was quickly pushed aside by the reality of becoming parents. It kept me up at night that my job paid fifteen dollars an hour and we had a baby on the way.

For strictly personal reasons, we were not budging on daycare. Too many co-workers, with kids catching endless array of ear infections and sicknesses, made us determined not to go in that direction. Adding to that was the expense. When we learned how much daycare cost, we concluded that the pay from one of our jobs would essentially just cover it.

Having Elizabeth stay home made family and financial sense, but it did not offset the dark reality we were staring at. Our child was due in mid-July, and when Elizabeth's maternity leave ended six weeks later, we would be a one-income family. The math wasn't hard to figure out: cutting our household income in half while adding a baby to the homestead equaled a yearly income of $32,000, down from the $60,000 income we currently had. Those numbers didn't factor in diapers, medicine, clothes, and whatever unexpected expenses come with a baby.

I entered full freakout mode. No matter how many emergency budget meetings we initiated, or how many ways I readjusted the numbers, it always looked the same. And by the same, I mean tight. Really tight. I assured my now very pregnant wife that we would be fine, but worry isn't an intense enough word to describe how I felt. 'Consumed with fear' is much closer. I would rather eat beans and rice every day than ask Elizabeth to stay at her job. I needed to figure something out.

It's Over

The low point came on a warm spring afternoon. We had been informed by our co-workers that when employees have their first baby, the company gives a nice pay increase to help out. My salary hovered somewhere around $32,000, while Elizabeth's was slightly lower. I was going nowhere fast financially with our normal three-percent increase, so the ten percent I heard bounced around gave me hope.

I entered my managing editor's office. He read my annual review, which was the best I had received since I started working there. I had just won Sports Photographer of the Year in the Pictures of the Year International contest, gaining fantastic national attention for myself, as well as our newspaper. My boss listed my accomplishments, then removed his glasses and rubbed his eyes before continuing.

"I did the best I could," he said, attempting to soften the blow. "You know it's been a tough year. Most employees didn't get any raise. I fought for you and got you three percent. I tried like hell to get you four percent, but there just isn't enough to go around."

We just stared at each other. My disappointment was obvious, but he didn't offer other options. "I'm sure three percent of your salary is a decent increase, but I hardly make anything. Three percent of nothing is still nothing," I replied defiantly.

"Let me see if I understand this," I continued. "No matter what I do, no matter how hard I work, no matter how many awards I win..."

I couldn't even finish what I was saying. A warm wave of heat rose through my body. I stood up from the comfortable chair that cost more than the raise I was going to receive. As I opened the door and stood underneath the doorframe, only two words came to my head.

It's over.

This career, as I knew it, was over. I walked like a zombie back to the photo department. As my co-workers joked about something, I sat at my desk to take in what just occurred. This wasn't just about the money—it was the realization that we would always struggle if we stayed. The dream career as a newspaper journalist was ideal for me before children, but unless I wanted to spend the next thirty years complaining like everyone else, I had to get out.

Where Do I Go from Here?

But where do I go from there? This was all I knew. If we were in a larger city, I could freelance more, but I knew a few freelance journalists in town, and we lived like kings compared to them. I had no idea what to do next, but I knew I needed to make more money.

There are certain moments where reality is impossible to ignore. I was a married, thirty-three-year-old man, making fifteen dollars an hour, with less than zero net worth, next to no money in the bank, and a baby on the way.

My new family deserved better than that.

So instead of cruising around town looking to make a photograph for the next day's paper, I went home to call my dad to see if I could pick up any temporary work within his business. I hadn't done any work for his company in a decade, but if I could pick up some side work during off-times, it could help withstand the blow.

My dad heard the fear in my voice. He had been there before.

He didn't sugarcoat what I was looking at. He could tell I was in a spot, but he didn't throw me a lifejacket either. What I was hoping for didn't line up with his business. So many things had changed since I last worked for him that I would need face-to-face training. That we lived fifteen hours apart made it impossible. I sat down on the bed, my body numb and my chest pounding. The hot afternoon sun streaming through the window onto my body only made things worse.

Like he did when he helped me find my career path ten years earlier, he offered a few simple questions that set me on a different course.

"Why would you want to work with me, anyway?" he asked. "You didn't like it when you worked for me last time."

I admitted it was only for the money.

"I think you should do what you know. You have a skill, but you aren't using that skill in the correct way. You need to start a side business. You've never wanted to do this, but why not shoot weddings?"

To a photojournalist, at least back then, shooting weddings was somewhere between being a J.C. Penney's portrait photographer and the clueless uncle who just bought his first camera.

Elizabeth and I both said we would never shoot a wedding. I had managed to avoid that horror for ten years, but there is something about feeding your newborn baby that smacks the arrogance out of your head. I got off the phone with a different mindset. I opened the phone book looking for local wedding photographers to call. Ten years earlier, when I started my photography career, I was in a similar situation, but I now had experience and confidence to fall back on. I'd never shot a wedding before, but I was sure these studios would see my years of experience as an asset.

My name had been under the bylines of photographs in the local newspaper for five years, but apparently, wedding photographers don't read the newspaper. I called multiple companies and none of them had any interest in talking with me. I was willing to be an assistant, or help in any way. I called two more smaller studios and received the same response. I threw the phone book against the wall in frustration. This was no longer a worry—this was now a challenge. I had finally gotten the motivation I so desperately needed. Every one of these companies flat-out rejected me. I was now too angry to be scared any longer.

I'm sure you've heard the phrase 'If you can't beat 'em, join 'em.' I flipped it around and had my inspiration.

If you can't join 'em, beat 'em.

And that's exactly what we set out to do. I suddenly saw this whole ordeal as a blessing. I hated traditional wedding photography. It was boring and stale. We were going to do things totally differently. We were going to do it with stories, emotion, and feeling, like we did with our photojournalism careers. And we were going to make the money we needed.

The energy flowed back into my downtrodden body. If we were going to do this, we were going to do it our way.

A New Beginning?

If it were only that easy.

Where do we begin? We'd never run a business before. Where would we find clients? How should we price our services? How do we figure out what our services are? There were a million questions we needed answered. I just knew we needed to get started.

We set out to create a portfolio. We had gone to a few friends' weddings where we took some photographs, and I had also photographed a small, intimate wedding for a newspaper assignment that year. That's all we had. With a collection of forty decent images from three weddings, we set out to launch a business. Our hopes were depressingly low. Neither of us had any business sense, and we obviously weren't awesome with money. But if we could make enough to cover diapers and the additional baby costs, we might keep our heads above water for a while.

We learned early on that clients often come from odd places. Fittingly, we were in our baby prep class, in the same building where our child would be born a few weeks later, when our teacher saw on our profile that we were photographers. She stopped us after class to ask if we knew anyone who shot weddings. Her daughter was looking for a photographer for her October wedding. Unlike our cold-feet response to the inquiries of the past, we jumped right on it. We exchanged information, but realized we didn't have a way to show our work. We hadn't even put together a website.

Realizing that we were being presented an awesome opportunity to get a running start, Elizabeth got busy that evening learning how to design a website. Heather, the bride-to-be, would be in town that weekend, so we set up a time to meet. That pushed up our timetable, but it also gave us a deadline. We needed her to see our work, and soon. Working day and night, Elizabeth somehow put together a bare bones site just in time.

Before we knew what hit us, we booked our first wedding. It wasn't for very much money, and we would both be working all day, but it was a start. With momentum and focus, we kept our eyes peeled for other couples looking for a last-minute photographer that year.

Within a month, we had booked three more weddings at rock-bottom prices.

Baby Time

Less than a week after depositing our very first business check, we visited Elizabeth's doctor to monitor the baby's progress. A routine appointment two weeks before the due date developed into a terrifying afternoon.

Concerned about the baby's health, the doctor questioned whether it was getting enough nutrients.

"We have to get the baby out," she suggested forcefully.

Elizabeth and I were both nervous and confused. She had been planning to do natural childbirth, but everything changed in an instant. When we asked questions about the negatives of a C-section, the doctor gave her cold assessment of the situation.

"We can wait, but I'd hate to have you come back next week and have a dead baby," were the remarkably chilling words that came out of her mouth.

That's all we needed to hear. Bedside manner be gone, she got her point across.

"Go home, pack your bags, and come back tonight. We'll induce and have a baby tomorrow," she said.

That was the moment—right there—when I turned into an adult. We were going to be parents tomorrow. No more planning. No more wondering. This was happening, and happening now.

As Elizabeth packed, I walked Lola while calling everyone important to relay the update. Elizabeth's mom booked a last-minute flight from Cleveland amid a hurricane blowing into Indiana. We made it to the hospital while the windows shook from the heavy winds. Sideway gusts rocked the building as doctors induced Elizabeth to prepare for surgery the next day. After a nearly sleepless night at home, I arrived at 5:30 a.m. to her wide awake while being attended to. The hurricane had blown past, but not before knocking out power throughout the area. Even though we had a name picked out for a boy and a girl, I almost had a change of heart after seeing the newspaper that morning.

The headline read *Tri-State Welcomes Dennis.*

How cool would it be to name him Dennis if he was a boy? On the day he was born, the newspaper would have welcomed him personally to the world! A word of advice to future dads-to-be: proposing a name change while your wife is in labor is similar to running outside during a hurricane. It's not going to end well.

"Dennis?" Elizabeth asked with a curious smile. "As in Dennis the Menace?"

So, okay, it wasn't going to be Dennis. I still thought that would have been cool. I guess I wasn't totally an adult yet. Considering the massive pain she was in and her lack of sleep, I was thoroughly impressed with how calmly she handled my juvenile request.

July 12th, 2005, went by in a blur, even though it was also excruciatingly long. It's painful to watch the person you love most go through such a physically and emotionally difficult time. While I was by her side, there was little I could do. At that same time, you are about to become parents, and there is nothing that prepares you for that overwhelming feeling.

What was supposed to be a morning birth was shifted to the afternoon. Even though the doctors induced her to prepare her body for childbirth, her body wasn't ready.

With my mother-in-law nervously waiting outside, I gave updates hourly. Frustration began setting in by 4:00 p.m. as Elizabeth continued to show little progress. That's when the conversation shifted to the possibility of a C-section as opposed to natural birth. It broke my heart to watch the doctors give Elizabeth the news, explaining that we were running out of time. The safety of the baby was at stake with her water being broken now for more than ten hours. Elizabeth understood and agreed, but now we were faced with a different dilemma. There weren't any operating rooms available. So, she waited. And waited. And waited.

Mercifully, around 7:30 p.m., a room became available. They prepped for surgery as the realization set in that she went through fourteen hours of labor and still had to undergo major abdominal surgery. This parenting thing was tough already, and we hadn't even held the little monkey yet.

There are so many moments you remember when your child is about to be born. It's like your body and mind go through a radical shift. Some things are blurry, and some things remain crystal clear. As I waited in the hallway while they prepped Elizabeth for surgery, I made sure I took a photograph of myself right before I went in to document the moment before I became a dad. My mother-in-law made fun of me while I snapped the image.

What really, truly shifted my brain was walking into the operating room. It wasn't what I expected. We had planned for Elizabeth to be in a big room with a comfortable bed and couches, but I was greeted by a tiny green room that seemed to get smaller each time I looked around. It was then that I asked myself a series of questions that startled me.

"This is the room? This is where we're going to become parents? Right here is where our life is going to change forever?"

It all moved so fast. Eight doctors, nurses, and anesthesiologists worked quickly yet meticulously while I could do nothing but rub Elizabeth's feet from under the blue cover. No words can accurately describe those minutes. The excitement, nervousness, and uncertainty built into my body would have given me the strength to run through those cold cinderblock walls. What was probably four minutes felt like a lifetime. Even though you don't know for sure, you can sense that they are close just by the words the doctors use, the tones of their voices, and the pauses at the important times. And then came the moment I will remember until my dying day.

The moment I heard our baby's voice for the first time. I couldn't see our child yet, but I sure could hear the little voice. The bellow from the tiny lungs announced the arrival like Hurricane Dennis the night before. From that moment on, we were now responsible for a human life.

The joy throughout the room truly made us feel that even the doctors and nurses had never experienced this before, even though they deliver babies every day. As they cleaned the baby and deftly put my wife back together, the doctor showed me our precious bundle for the first time— and put me on the spot with a question I needed to answer correctly.

"Dad, do you want to tell Mom if it's a boy or a girl?"

Anyone in the know can verify that newborn babies in real life do not look like newborn babies in the movies. They just don't. There are chords and stuff and things and, in the moment, it still seems like a work in progress. So, I assessed the situation and took what seemed to be an educated guess.

"It's a... boy?" I said not so confidently.

The doctors confirmed my answer as our celebration began, although it wasn't Dennis we welcomed to the Tri-State. It was Andrew. There is a picture from that night that holds my attention. As Elizabeth finally got rest after returning to our room, my mother-in-law took a photograph of Andrew and me.

That Photograph

That photograph is why I finally decided to write this book. This is for every new parent who will be in that same moment, or for those who want a better family life with your children going forward. The decisions that you make with your money and your time are so vitally important from that moment on. All of a sudden, the way we handle money has such a greater importance, and so many fathers miss it. My experience as a fifteen-year-old—and the horrible memories of that ordeal—shaped my mindset on money, business, and family in a way that is still with me today. I am eternally grateful for those horrible memories. Without those memories, I never would have learned such valuable lessons. And they are lessons that so many more in our culture are going to learn the hard way. Having control of your money isn't a greed thing—it's a successful life thing.

My parents instilled in me very early the value of work and the value of earning our own money. When I was ten, a car commercial appeared on our television screen. As my brother Steve and I "oohed" and "aahed" over the slick red vehicle, my dad saw it as a great learning experience. Getting up from the couch, he turned off the television as soon as the commercial ended.

"I want to let the both of you know that your mom and I will not be buying you a car. So, if you're going to want a car, you're going to save up and buy it yourselves."

He turned the television back on, leaving us to ponder his words. The following summer, I was delivering newspapers. The next winter, I hesitantly dressed as Santa Claus to wave to passing motorists along Willis Avenue. The embarrassment vastly multiplied when my friends at school found out it was me inside that smelly suit. I added a few odd jobs, and by fourteen, had amassed a nice little bank account. When I took a job as a busboy at the Howard Johnson's restaurant within walking distance of my home, the money started to get real.

After all, having control of your money affects every area of your life. The lack of money—or rather the lack of control over money—destroyed the relationship I had with my father for a decade. It killed the dreams he had of sending me to college. It drove our family to the brink of bankruptcy. But in every hardship, there comes a valuable lesson to learn.

I learned the value of controlling your money from a young age. I felt firsthand the devastating damage that debt in life can do to a family. And I knew that when I eventually did have a family, money was going to be a blessing, not a curse.

When we found out Elizabeth was pregnant, my childhood memories flooded back into my brain. Realizing that I had allowed debt to slowly creep into our lives—almost the same exact amount of debt that was thrown onto my parents—I went into attack mode. I decided to attack the debt we had before our son was born, the way my dad did after all the heartache. My father's experience is the primary reason for our success. His lessons taught me to despise debt. And it gave me a front-row seat to a real-life financial crisis that set me on the course to freedom.

We are all shaped by our respective pasts. Our future depends on what we do with the lessons learned. When I saw that adorable little son of ours for the first time, I was determined to do everything in my power to never allow anything like that to happen to us.

What my family went through was abnormal, but what is now normal is the steady, treacherous collection of debt that new families voluntarily assume.

Simply put, debt limits choices and adds stress. Taking on a car payment, some student loans, and a little credit card debt might seem manageable when you are only responsible for yourself. But as a married couple, two car payments, multiple student loans, credit cards, and then a mortgage are enough to strain any relationship beyond repair. Any job loss can send the family into a frightening financial spiral.

And instead of overwhelming feelings of joy, the arrival of a new baby brings up serious talks about daycare, money issues, and the overall stress that comes from the lack of family time. This isn't the way most new parents envision their parenting years, yet it's becoming increasingly common.

A New Start

With our first child on the way—and all the uncertainty that comes with it—we pressed pause on the debt snowball. We went into money-hibernation mode until after Andrew was born, but when we strapped our tiny, 5 lb., 8 oz. baby boy securely into his car seat for the brief, two-minute drive home, I was nerdy enough to make sure an important voice greeted him when we started the car.

Dave Ramsey's show played on the radio as we drove slower than everyone else west on Washington Avenue. It was a symbolic gesture to greet the start of his life to let him know that we were going to do everything we could to teach him the right way. You can laugh at my silliness, but I state it proudly because we were that intense about getting in great financial shape.

Everyone advised us to get sleep whenever possible, and they unknowingly scared us into believing we would turn into zombies. It turned out to be easier than we anticipated. Having a baby who is a good sleeper is vital when deciding to have more children. A challenging first baby is a candidate for an only child.

Since he began sleeping four to six hours a night within a few weeks, we began to get our legs beneath us again. I went back to work at the paper, plotting the opening steps of our business and freaking about money again. The clock was ticking on Elizabeth's employment. She hadn't quit her job, but that eventual result was a forgone conclusion. It was just a matter of when. It was a race to see if we could turn this business into something profitable before she was forced to make a decision.

The Foundation

There were many times during the debt snowball when we questioned whether it would work. It's difficult to sacrifice your lifestyle when there is no immediate reward. You see your friends traveling, buying new cars, eating out, and moving into bigger houses.

In reality, we were in the very beginning of building the foundation. When you watch the construction of a skyscraper, it's hard to believe that what is just a hole now will eventually be a building one hundred stories in the air. So, to build a solid foundation, you need to dig down before you build up. You need to clear out all the mess from your past before you can build your future.

The most disturbing part of the beginning of our journey was the pushback we received from nearly every corner of our personal society. When we became convinced we could live without debt, we were blindsided by the resistance from people close to us. We expected it from our younger friends who have never experienced life without debt, but when I noticed older people discouraging us, I realized how deeply being in debt has become a cultural norm.

When we turned down requests for vacations or social events, we were met with the phrase "You only live once" more times than I can count. We were weird enough to know that spending money didn't mean going somewhere we didn't care to go just to fit into the YOLO model. Elizabeth and I told each other in private that eventually we'd be able to vacation wherever and whenever we wanted—and we wouldn't do it with debt.

The debt culture is so normal that the sooner you embrace how uncommon you are by getting out of debt, the sooner you will envision your exceedingly bright future. You will get resistance, and you will get made fun of—often by those closest to you—but in five or ten years, when you are living a life of freedom, they will be the same people who will tell you that you're lucky.

Accept it. Embrace it. Make it your badge of honor.

Building the Skyscraper

By the fall of 2005, we had booked four weddings and were cautiously optimistic about being able to eat something better than dog food once we were down to one "real" income. We offered discounts and incentives to anyone who even mumbled the words "wedding photographer."

Elizabeth's maternity leave ended, but due to complications from the delivery, she was unable to go back to work full-time. This was when being a sweetheart like she is paid off. The higher-ups allowed her to keep her position—unpaid—without having to formally quit. Even though we were dead set against her going back full-time, there was comfort in knowing that the job was still there if we absolutely needed it.

While I worked at the paper, Elizabeth used Andrew's sleeping time to design our new website and do the tasks related to growing the business. It was a tumultuous few months, filled with uncertainty, stress, and a slight sense that we were onto something. The wedding photography industry was filled with hobbyists who copied each other's poses. We set out to be the anti-wedding photographers.

When we first thought of starting the business, we knew we had a product that was different. Two-photographer wedding packages are now common, if not expected. Twelve years ago, it was relatively unheard of. The fact that Elizabeth and I were both experienced photojournalists added to our advantage. Most wedding photographers learn photography while shooting weddings, which is frightening when you think about the quality of work produced for their first batch of clients.

Elizabeth and I had the advantage of years of daily, in-the-trenches shooting while being critiqued by seasoned veterans. We never planned on running a business, so we never thought the professional and artistic growth we achieved would be used for anything but a job. This was what my dad was trying to teach me when he said I had a skill, but wasn't using it wisely. We were much more marketable than we realized. But our salaries told us otherwise.

When we delivered the wedding images to our first clients, we were stunned by the overwhelming reaction. We realized immediately that we had unearthed a hidden gem. In other words, our acre of diamonds, which we will discuss later in the book. We charged them what is considered the low-end of the industry, and even that was a considerable increase over the money we made at the newspaper. We busted it for all those years to be better newspaper photographers, never realizing the skills we developed would be applicable—and more profitable—in another area.

Red 'X'

The late nights were about to begin. We needed to learn a whole new business, and there was a learning curve in every direction. To say we were overwhelmed would be a severe understatement. Elizabeth and I couldn't have a conversation without it somehow relating back to the business.

Each night, after Elizabeth and Andrew fell asleep, I stayed up doing more research. I felt the need to study the competition. Their prices. The services they offered. The quality of their work and their website. The text they used, the graphics they designed, and the brand they portrayed.

I couldn't help but envy many of the photographers I studied throughout the country. They had already built what we desired to have. During one of those blurry-eyed evenings, I noticed one photographer who had a calendar on his site showing the dates he had already booked. He also had high-end prices and a booked wedding season. As I scrolled through the available dates, I got to the winter months and noticed something that boggled my mind. He had placed a red 'x' over every date in December. There was also a note that declared he was not accepting any work in the month of December. Why? So he could enjoy the holidays with his family.

Um, what? You can do that? This guy had built his business so solid he had the guts to close off an entire month on his calendar? In my scarcity mindset, all I thought about was how much money he was leaving on the table. I calculated the dollar amount he turned away if he booked just two weddings and six corporate shoots, which wouldn't be odd in December. I could not relate to turning away that amount of cash, but I also wasn't living his life. Can you imagine the power to turn away all that work—I mean everything—around the holidays so you could enjoy family time?

After listening to so many struggling photographers tell me how the market was oversaturated and there was no money in it anymore, this guy gave me hope. It planted the seeds of what our future would look like if we could control our schedule even half as well as he did.

Seeing the Dream

During our first year in business, we caught a glimpse of the future we desired. It looked an awful lot like what I just described.

Arriving at the bride's home one sunny morning, I was immediately struck by the atmosphere inside. The family bond was unmistakable. Laura, the bride, glided toward the kitchen while her sister and mom waited with smiles. The love they had for each other flowed effortlessly. Photographing them while they finished their makeup, I caught a glimpse of a large vehicle in their back window.

"Is that an R.V.?" I asked passively, meant to provide little more than small talk.

Their eyes lit up and their smiles grew wider. They traded telling the story, cutting each other off with perfect timing. Laura explained how her dad ran his own business. He bought the R.V. when she was ten. Laura's younger sister then mentioned how, every summer, he would shut down his business for a month so they could travel the country together.

"They were the most wonderful times together," Laura reminisced. "Each trip made us closer to each other, and we got to see every part of the country. Those are my favorite memories."

I had just read somewhere that the greatest thing you can give your child is wonderful memories.

It wasn't long before their dad walked into the kitchen, planting a kiss on each of their heads. His confident demeanor, impressive head of grayish hair, and firm handshake grabbed my full attention. Along with the story I just heard, I was immediately impressed.

"How in the world can someone shut down their business for a month to travel with their family?" was the question I kept asking myself on my way to the chapel where Laura was to be married to her fiancé, Julian.

I left thinking that was the coolest thing their father did. We were broke as a joke, working two full-time jobs, and starting a business we didn't know would succeed. Still, I left invigorated. While I photographed their wedding, I watched how close that family was with each other. I still see the father-daughter dance and Laura's beaming smile for her dad. I wanted that for our family.

It sounded so freeing to have the ability to do what he did. It was even more impressive that he actually did it. I knew people with the ability to shut down a month every year to travel with their family, but they always had a reason not to. But he didn't. He actually did it. He created the bond. He fostered their strong relationship. He allowed those memories to happen. And now, even as she was leaving to start a life and a family of her own, they were closer than ever. They still travel together, and plan to in the future. For them, it wasn't going to end—but only because they put the time in early to create that relationship.

Could we do that? That thought dominated my mind in the days that followed. We wouldn't travel now, of course. Andrew was too young to remember any of it. There was also the fact that we didn't have any money. We had loads of debt we were fighting to pay off. I had a job I was trying to get out of and a business we were fighting to build. But I couldn't stop asking myself that question over and over.

Could we do that?

It became our dream. Not only for the travel, but for the freedom it represented. Having the ability to decide to take a month—or three—without asking anyone else's permission was the type of life we desired.

The Value of Our Time

On my way to work the following Monday, I thought about what went into going to my job every day. Alarm clock, shower, getting dressed, driving, work—at least an eight-hour time commitment, plus the drive home. I got to work and calculated how much money I was paid for an entire day. I ran the numbers three times to make sure they were correct.

For every one of those days, I brought home $96.20. Ninety-six dollars! Oh, and twenty cents. Including the time to get ready and get home, I was trading eleven hours for less than $100. The number is slightly skewed because it doesn't include the health care benefits and my minuscule 401(k) contributions, but it was easy to figure out why we had been struggling financially. It wasn't the money, it was the time. Making $100 wasn't killing us, but giving up eleven hours to do so was.

I always heard about the value of hard work, but I don't remember hearing much about the value of time. I did hear often that "time is money," but it looked like I didn't really listen. When we finally made the association that our time was more valuable than the money we were paid, I knew that not only did I want to get out of that job, I had to get out of that job.

Knowing that we charged the industry low for our first wedding, there was tremendous room for growth. And we could see that even if we continued to charge low prices, we would still make more money and spend less time working than we did at the newspaper. With only two other weddings booked, I was ready to quit right there. But we wanted to be out of debt before we went out on our own. And we still owed on a car payment, student loan and mortgage.

It was around this time that it started clicking in our minds. Even though being completely debt free was a few years away, we could taste what that life might be like.

I started to daydream about what could happen. If we paid off our home, the monthly income we needed to survive would be slashed by thirty percent. If we could figure out this business a little better and raise our prices just to industry norms, we would surpass our current income by photographing thirty weddings—as opposed to working a combined 450 days per year. Talk about taking control of our time!

That didn't mean we would only work thirty days to make up that money. There were meetings, post-production, and other business details, but we could do most of that from our home on our own time. That word 'freedom' kept popping into my head, over and over and over. And not just time freedom, which I began to lay out for you above, but financial freedom.

What would it be like to not owe anybody a dime? What would it be like to work on our business and not somebody else's? What would it feel like to wake up every morning and have complete control over what we did and accomplished?

I would get so giddy thinking about it that my knee would bounce. Literally. I sat back and wished I would have learned this when I was twenty (but, of course, I knew everything back then). Fortunately, I had another chance, and there was no way I was going to let it slip away. The idea of becoming a 'nerd' had never been so cool. I watched co-workers walk into work every day with slouched shoulders and no passion. It was a job—nothing more—and they had no way out. That time for us was over. I knew that if all our projections came true, I would be at the job for two years before we were ready to go out on our own.

The Big Plan

We would be living on one income from the newspaper, plus whatever money we made from the business. So, Elizabeth and I came up with the ambitious, if not self-mutilating idea, of living off our newspaper income alone and putting every penny we made from the business toward paying down our debt. My thinking was this: the quicker we grow the business, the sooner we would be out of debt. The quicker we were out of debt, the sooner we could quit the job and be on our own. The idea wasn't to be wedding photographers—it was to live a life of freedom. Wedding photography was simply our quickest route.

But to make this work, not a penny of the income from the business could be used for anything but paying off our debt. The business would grow from hustle and word of mouth, and we would use only the equipment we had. We couldn't grab a chunk for a quick vacation or buy a refrigerator. Aside from buying books and investment in personal growth, we held off on every other unneeded expense. The short-term sacrifices would be worth it once we exited the tunnel into the light of freedom. We were becoming debt free. Everything else could wait.

And as my wife would tell you, it did. Our friends and family thought we had lost our ever-loving minds. We jumped on the crazy train. We turned down doing everything. EVERYTHING. No vacations. Even going out to dinner was as rare as an uncooked steak. Home improvements were a thing of the past or the future, but certainly not the present. Master bathrooms remained outdated and wardrobes stayed the same. The time for action had arrived.

A Midwest Advantage?

Now, I can hear the grumbling from the East and West Coast folks as I type.

$140,000 of debt, including your house? Bwah. Houses are going for half a mil in my neighborhood. It's not possible to do that out here.

First off, I hear you. The cost of living and hefty taxes were one of the reasons I left New York.

But secondly, recall that we lived on a salary of $32,000. If you chart our income-to-debt ratio, it would be remarkably similar to a basic Bay Area or Big Apple household income, and the freelance rates in those markets are three times what we could command in the Midwest.

This formula, we discovered, can work anywhere.

Deposits of Failure

With our budget stretched tighter, there wasn't room for error. My false bravado of having to prove myself was the only thing keeping me from stressing about what the future would look like if our business failed. If we allowed ourselves to think about what could go wrong, we would have accepted our fate and slid back into our day jobs, believing our excuses about how it was too hard to pull off. And nobody would have blamed us, either. We weren't burning through cheerleader applications.

Starting a business, particularly a first business, can be mentally and physically all-consuming. Personally, I have the ability to overthink anything, and something of this magnitude can take over. But no amount of information can replace experience, a lesson we learned the hard way. How does that saying go? When a person with money meets a person with experience, the person with money gains experience and the person with experience gains the money. Ouch. So true.

In our first full year in business, we scored a victory with our highest-priced wedding to date. We were so thrilled to get it that we adjusted many of the terms in our contract to fit the couples' wants. We added hours to sweeten the deal. We added a complimentary engagement session. We gave a credit for a wedding album. We would do whatever it took. What we didn't change was our rock bottom retainer amount. The retainer to secure the wedding date was $250, which is a paltry amount to hold a date for a $3,500 wedding more than a year in advance. The second and third payments, due prior to the wedding, would be where almost all the money came in. But the low retainer made it easy for the couple to book the date.

But every rose has its thorn. Usually multiple thorns. A week after the second payment was due, I called the mother of the bride to remind her about the late payment. We had depended on these two checks, being our two biggest of the year. She casually informed me that a family member had graciously offered to do the photography as a gift to the couple. This apparently had been decided months before without us being in the loop. I mentioned that we had a signed contract together and had turned away every inquiry for this date for nearly a year. Her second payment was already past due.

"Sorry," she said curtly, and hung up the phone.

Just like that, we were out more than $3,000. I'm not sure what your financial situation is like, but three grand was a big, hairy deal to us. It threw us into a complete panic. Elizabeth and I scheduled another one of our emergency late-night meetings. I was furious, hurt, and scared at the same time. I worried that this would happen over and over. This wasn't something we had ever anticipated. We lost the money, but we gained experience. Even though we fretted about raising our retainer, we knew it was the next step. If someone wasn't going to book us because our retainer was too high, we would have to let them go. And letting go of clients who were willing to pay us wasn't comfortable. That was the night we had to accept our new reality:

Get comfortable being uncomfortable.

Super Opportunity

I was fully on board—and most of the time driving—the freedom train. Through the winter crossover from 2005 to 2006, I watched as my favorite football team, the Pittsburgh Steelers, finished out the regular season with four straight victories while grabbing the final postseason spot. The Steelers won the Super Bowl when I was seven and eight years old, and one of my childhood dreams was to see them play in a Super Bowl in person.

I preached the frugal life to Elizabeth, and that was about to smack me in the back of the head. Pittsburgh finished an improbable playoff run and advanced to Super Bowl XL. Downstairs at our bar, I stared at the laptop exploring Super Bowl ticket prices, and it wasn't pretty. Before the Steelers had won, a single ticket could be had for $1,200, but the prices increased quickly.

And just so I'm crystal clear, we had the money. And logistics worked in my favor. The Super Bowl was in Detroit, an eight-hour drive from our home. Unlike past Super Bowls in California, Arizona, or Louisiana, I wouldn't need to purchase a flight ticket, rental car, or multiple nights at a hotel.

I had the fever, and Elizabeth grew wary. I knew I had to lay it out in perfect form if I didn't want to lose her trust. I explained that the cost of the ticket would be the only real expense. I was fine getting in the car Super Bowl morning. I was fine making the drive and parking far from the stadium to save money. I was fine eating Arby's after the game and staying in a cheap motel in Toledo. I just wanted to be at the game.

After a week of heavy pressure, Elizabeth finally gave her cautious approval. I could see in her eyes that she was disappointed I was willing to spend that much money on a ticket to one football game while we needed to cut everything else in our life to get out of debt. But when I poured on the guilt that they hadn't won a Super Bowl in twenty-five years and who knew if I would ever get that chance again, she went along with it. We made a deal that I wouldn't pay more than $2,000 for a ticket.

By the time I was ready to buy, tickets had jumped over the $2,000 range. She bit her tongue while I went online multiple times a day to find a deal. All it would take would be for one person to panic and drop the price and I was ready to buy. The cheapest ticket stayed around $2,200 as I tried to get an increase from the wife. She reminded me of the deal we made.

Finally, after days and days of scouring ticket prices online, I found a single ticket for $1,899. I called Elizabeth to confirm, and with a quiet voice, she gave her approval. I was going to the Super Bowl! It had all lined up perfectly. All I needed to do was press the button to purchase the coveted ticket.

But I couldn't do it.

Something inside prevented me from buying the one ticket I had wanted my entire life. I tried to rationalize that someday, when we were loaded, I wouldn't miss that money. And I was pretty sure that would be true at some point. But right now, it just didn't feel right. It felt like I was abandoning the plan I had so fervently set forth. I thought about how much of a hypocrite I would be the following week when I was back to being the budget Nazi. I envisioned the resentment in my wife's eyes when I preached sacrifice to get to our dream life. "Sacrifice," she would think, "unless it's something you really want."

On February, 5th, 2006, while the Steelers played for the world championship in Detroit, I watched the game in our living room with Elizabeth, Andrew, our friend Justin, and our little puppy at my feet. The Steelers won their fifth world championship, their first since I was eight years old.

After we celebrated and Justin went home, I went downstairs to our bar to watch the post-game celebration. Instead of feeling euphoria that my favorite team had once again reached the pinnacle, I felt somber. I was totally bummed out that I was in the basement instead of being in Detroit enjoying what looked to be an incredible celebration. The whole thing wasn't about the Steelers or a football game—it was about experiences. Seeing the Steelers win a championship in person was something I always wanted to experience, and I missed out. The only solace I had was that I was at home with my family where I should be and had not abandoned them or our plan.

The Pushback

To nobody's surprise, weddings happen on Saturdays, and newspapers publish every day of the week, so we had a big problem. Elizabeth and I had booked twenty-five weddings for 2006, and the majority of them were scheduled on a day where I would be working at the paper. This would be no easy feat to navigate. It was also a touchy subject since Saturdays are precious days off for all of us.

At first, it went smoothly. Our schedule had a pattern to it, so I could see which months I would be scheduled to work on those wedding days. Our newspaper staff was close-knit, and it was common to make sacrifices for each other. I was able to change dates for the first few months without angering anyone—until our boss caught wind of how many dates I had switched. Then I ran into a big problem.

Calling me into his office, he informed me he wasn't happy with what was going on. He had a good point since I knew this wasn't sustainable. He asked how many weddings we were shooting that year. When he heard the number, he laughed and shook his head the way my dad would do when I asked to borrow the car.

"There is no way you're getting all those Saturdays off," he informed me. He then asked a question I hadn't thought of. "What if everyone here decided to shoot weddings on the side? Why should you get the choice to have all these Saturdays off?"

It was a very good question, and I didn't have a very good answer. I guess it wasn't fair. Being that all the photographers laughed at us when we started with the wedding thing, I assumed we were the only ones interested. But now we had a big problem: if I couldn't get a Saturday switched, I would not be allowed to call in sick because they already knew I had requested the day off. If I didn't show up, it was grounds for termination.

Week by week, we hung by a tightrope. If someone could not switch in advance—or worse—someone changed their mind last minute, we were up a creek without a paddle. Nearly every Saturday that wedding season we faced the possibility of either having to back out of a wedding and destroy the reputation of our new business or me getting fired from my job.

Elizabeth and I had long, stressed-out conversations about this all season long. We agreed that we had to keep our word with the wedding clients we booked. I couldn't justify backing out of such an important day for any couple just to save my job. I made this bed; now I had to lie in it.

Late one summer night, while swatting away mosquitoes on our backyard deck, we finally came to the conclusion that if the newspaper insisted I had to work on a wedding Saturday, I would quit, or be fired. That was scary to say out loud. We didn't say it with a victory smile. We said it while fighting back fear and hoping upon hope that it did not come to that. We certainly didn't feel prepared to go out on our own. But we felt this was more of our future than the newspaper, so we had to hope we were making the right decision.

Job Sharing

I was exhausted as I prepared for work one morning. The wedding I shot the previous Saturday kicked my butt, and my sleep tank was empty. Elizabeth was still on unpaid leave from the newspaper. As I got my cameras together, I looked at her playing with Andrew and made a comment to her out of envy.

"Why don't you go to work for me today so I can be home with Andrew?" I said with a combination of sarcasm and exhaustion. Her reply intrigued me.

"I'd do that for you," she said. "I'd even go in a couple days a week. You'd get more time with Andrew, and I'd get out of the house, get to shoot, and see everyone."

We looked at each other with curiosity. Was that even possible? Technically, she was still employed there, and they loved her. The only reason they kept Elizabeth on leave was that they were hoping she would return to work. Upon entering the office that morning, I made an impromptu stop at the managing editor's office.

"Can Elizabeth and I share a job?" was all I asked.

My boss gave me the same look Elizabeth did. He was curious, as well, but he had no idea if it was possible.

"Nobody has ever tried that before, but I love the idea," he stated. "Besides, we like Elizabeth better than you anyway!"

I'd never been so happy to be insulted. At least he said it with a smile. Before lunch, we huddled up in the human resources department, attempting to sort out the details. Surprisingly, there were no policies, politics, or opponents of the idea to hold it back. We would be vacating one job, giving them the opportunity to rehire for the position. It would also mean there wouldn't be the option for both of us to work full-time again. They thought we would have a problem with that. We saw that as the next step to freedom. The following week, Elizabeth and I were sharing a job. And I had my first taste of time freedom.

Depending on our workload within the business, I would work three or four days at the paper, and Elizabeth would work one or two days. It was an ideal agreement for everyone. I got a break from the relentless pace I'd brought on myself, and Elizabeth got just enough of the work and socializing that went away when Andrew was born. And the newspaper got Elizabeth back in some form, allowing them to rehire for her position. It re-enforced in my mind that there is always a solution if you think long enough, hard enough, and consult the right people.

Purple Daddy Eater

Not long after the paperwork was filed, that agreement paid off for me big time. Dressed for work and ready to walk out of the door, I wanted to make Andrew laugh before I left. I grabbed a toy—a long-stemmed flower with a suction cup on the other end—which attached to his high-chair. Sitting on the floor next to him, I took the flower and suctioned it directly to my forehead. I waved my head back and forth, and his giggles and laughs increased with the speed of the flower. Elizabeth, sitting a few feet away, shook her head and smiled.

After the cheap laughs were exhausted, I went to pull the flower off my forehead. I thought I'd create a grand finale by ripping it off quickly. As I did, I felt a rush toward the top of my head. Elizabeth's mouth opened in a stunned fashion. Tears welled up in her eyes. I could tell by her reaction—and Andrew's stare—that something went terribly wrong. I jumped up quickly to a mirror. What was reflected back to me had to be a joke. I had managed to give myself a giant, deep purple hickey in the center of my forehead. This wasn't a tiny bruise. This was a full-blown circle that covered a third of my forehead. And I was expected at work in ten minutes.

Elizabeth was now laughing so hard she couldn't breathe. I was running around the house in hysterics unable to process a rational thought. This thing is not going away anytime soon. I can't cover it with a hat. I can't hide it with anything. I guess I could have gone all Bret Michaels and done the bandana and cowboy hat thing, but I didn't have the materials or guts to pull it off.

"I cannot go out in public like this!" I screamed into the mirror.

And then I realized we're job-sharing now. Elizabeth's laughter subsided quickly when she realized she needed to go to work for me. My stupid stunt cost her the next few days at home with Andrew. Fortunately, with a decent amount of healing and a heavy dose of makeup, I was able to shoot the wedding we had scheduled that Saturday. I was finally able to laugh at myself when I saw the color theme for that wedding was purple. How appropriate.

About That Gold Watch...

The newspaper staff gathered in the triangular conference room to bid farewell to a longtime employee. After thirty-five years, Larry, a co-worker, was retiring from his job as copy editor. One of the cards written to him proudly claimed "Now it's time to start living!"

It seemed so odd to work in a job for your entire adult life so you could then start living. A few dozen employees gathered for cake, stories, and a good old-fashioned sendoff. Larry worked the nightshift, kept quiet, and stared at a screen while he was at work, so very few of the stories regarded him or his long career.

The room was filled with small talk and a depressing discussion about more corporate buyouts.

This soft-spoken man reluctantly stood next to the newspaper's editor to accept his congratulations and the gold watch that was a gift from the company. The gold watch has long been the gift of choice to appreciate an employee's loyalty and dedication. We clapped as he pushed his glasses off the middle of his nose to open the watch. After he opened it, he read the congratulatory engraving on the back.

The room full of co-workers gasped in disbelief. His name had been printed incorrectly.

It took thirty-five years to attain the gold watch. Maybe he needed forty years to have his name spelled correctly. It confirmed to me even more how much I needed to get out.

Labor Pains

The impatience for getting out of debt intensified as we navigated the rocky terrain of a new business. Licenses, insurance, and other details filled up the minimal time we had between day job and our new little family. Elizabeth and I realized quickly that our education prepared us for being an employee, but hardy for self-employment. We learned quickly that making photographs was going to be a small part of what it took to run a successful photography business. Business books piled up on the nightstand as our new education began. We needed to prepare quickly for a world we weren't prepared for. Starting a new business comes with mistakes, and we were no exception.

Our first full year was filled with rookie mistakes, from pricing blunders to customer-relations snafus. Our retainers were too low. Our contracts were too vague. We spent too much money on advertising and too much time at meetings. We would let the customer dictate when and where we would have those meetings, and often they didn't show up. After expenses and equipment, our profit was low while our time investment was high.

My impatience for getting out of debt only fueled the frustrations of the initial business launch. Even though the progress was normal and ahead of schedule, I put pressure on the situation by focusing intensely on how much money we owed on the car, student loan, and house. I continued to consume *The Dave Ramsey Show* daily and study the callers' mistakes. It was uncanny how many topics seemed to be directly related to what we were struggling with. It became the daily business and money course we didn't get in college.

As winter slowly turned to spring, we witnessed some of the fruits of our labor taking shape. With an April surge in bookings, our season filled up. By mid-summer, we had paid off the car and the student loan. Our next big financial goal was to get our mortgage balance below $100,000, but we couldn't crack that elusive number.

But once we finally pushed the balance into five figures, the momentum shift took place. We could see that this was leading us where we needed to go. We kept telling ourselves that this was the hard part. We were either going to pay now or pay later, and we wanted to rip the Band-Aid off as quickly as possible.

We anticipated money being tight as we continued to put every dime of business money into the mortgage, but we were woefully unprepared for how tight time would become. I have a tendency to underestimate the amount of time that goes into a project. Maybe it's because I didn't want to get discouraged and give up, or maybe it's because I had a poor understanding of details, but we found ourselves trapped by our own schedule at the end of the wedding season.

We were behind on getting the photographs to our clients, and with the job at the newspaper and our little baby, there was no other time to pull from. Elizabeth and I had multiple bleary-eyed, late-night conversations about how long we could burn the candle at both ends without getting our fingers scorched. It was a high-wire act that I was more comfortable with than she was. Being the numbers guy, I saw the progress we were making. By the end of 2006, we had paid more than $30,000 toward our mortgage and had a balance of less than $70,000 when we once again fell asleep before the ball dropped on New Year's Eve.

Elizabeth felt the pain of our plan much more than I did. She had a husband who was hard-charging but increasingly inattentive. She was swamped with excess work from the business that wasn't in our life a year earlier. And she was caring for our one-year-old with little sleep and decreasing patience. The candle was burning faster.

An Escape Clause?

As the cracks in the newspaper's foundation grew deeper and thicker, rumors of buyouts circulated. If they didn't get enough volunteers to take the buyouts, layoffs could follow. Everyone around me went into panic mode. No matter how good the severance numbers were, nobody I talked to was prepared to take it. I, on the other hand, was excited. This was a nightmare to them, but it would be a dream come true for me. You want to pay me to quit? You are offering me a big check to walk away? Where do I sign up?

So, I called down to Human Resources to set up a meeting. I went home and calculated my years of service and my salary to get a ballpark figure of what offer I might expect. It wouldn't have taken a huge number to get me to bite. A few months of paid salary would give me the running start I needed to go for it. I walked into HR with a big smile and a hopeful mind.

I didn't waste time. I let them know immediately that I was interested in taking the buyout and asked what they would be able to offer. The two HR employees laughed, and waited for my real question. I didn't laugh back. Maybe it's a negotiating tactic, I thought.

"Vince," one of them asked, already knowing what my answer would be. "How old are you?"

"Thirty-five," I said.

"Buyouts are only offered to employees fifty-five and over," he responded.

"Oh," I said with confused disappointment. "Why?"

They laughed again and explained that it's the company policy. I questioned the purpose of the policy. Why do I need to work here longer for them to want to get rid of me? If they were offering buyouts, why not take one from someone who truly wanted it without having to lay someone off?

They agreed it was a good question, and then told me to come back in twenty years.

The Year of Work

With my short-lived buyout dream squashed, we dug in.

When I look back on our life, family, and business, 2007 was the turning point in many ways. This was the year our business took off. We booked thirty-nine weddings that year. I continued to work full-time at the newspaper while chasing our two-year-old around the house. And why not add another baby to the family while we were at it? Elizabeth became pregnant right around the New Year, and our second baby was scheduled to arrive in September, which already had every Saturday booked with weddings.

Trouble Ahead

This was, without question, the most difficult year of this process. We knew it would be crazy, but we didn't know it would be that crazy. We completely over scheduled ourselves with no way to turn back. If our plan to become debt free is something you wish to follow, this is where I would tell you we went too far. We sold out big time for the goal, and we soon realized we bit off more than we could chew.

Between the job and the business, there was barely a day off from work that year. Most down-time was spent on the back-end work of the business, and the stress fell firmly upon our marriage. Our first wedding to photograph was three days into the year, and the work never slowed down. There were thirty-eight more weddings to shoot, on top of the job. The problems began with a lack of sleep. It quickly grew toward occasional passive-aggressive sarcasm. We then argued constantly.

We had no choice but to take a deep breath, hold each other's hands, and work through what was ahead of us. We dubbed it 'The Year of Work'. We knew we had to be prepared. The workload we took on wasn't going to change, and we knew that it could tear at the fibers of our marriage if we allowed it. An emotional, pregnant mom is not the ideal person to push when it comes to time, sleep, and life, but leave it to me to try. I was exhaustedly excited. My empathy glands obviously weren't fully developed yet at thirty-six years old. Elizabeth just wanted some sleep.

Despite the struggles, 'The Year of Work' had moments of positive, cornerstone memories.

Each Saturday, as Elizabeth and I packed our equipment for the wedding of the week, one of the four babysitters we relied upon would pull up to our house. I would look out the window to see a beautiful, metallic-blue sports car, or some days, a red convertible gleaming in the sunlight. Next to that car were our two clunkers, ready for battle. I had a proud moment as I looked at the contrast in vehicles.

"I know we're on the right track," I professed to Elizabeth as we carried the cameras to our cars. "When our babysitter is driving a better car than us, we're on the right track." One day, we would be able to drive whatever we wanted without a payment attached to it.

It took many of these moments for us to become hardened to the pressures of our social circle. We knew we were odd a year earlier when we set off on a canoeing trip with a large group of friends. Everyone gathered at our house before we hit the road. In front of our house were ten new vehicles, almost all black, each looking newer than the other. The last car in that convoy was Elizabeth's unattractive green Saturn, which was the ugly duckling of the swans in front. I took it as a badge of honor, even though our friends had to have thought we were broke.

When the engine in my Saturn unexpectedly bit the dust, we had a decision to make. My brother asked if I thought about replacing the engine. I didn't know that was possible. Since everything else in the car seemed fine, I searched around. Within a week, I found a used engine with 39,000 miles on it for a little over $1,000. They would install it, as well. Like a heart replacement from a twenty-year-old into a fifty-year-old body, I was back on the road in a week, and our path to financial freedom barely hit a snag.

The ego hit of driving older cars wasn't hard to adjust to. The exhaustion of endless work and hardly any rest was much more difficult. Twice in 2007, we booked triple wedding weekends, which were financially wonderful, but stupid in every other way. When we shoot one wedding per weekend, it requires the next day to physically bounce back. Doubles are tough. Triples are insane.

The first triple was on Memorial Day weekend, and I get tired just thinking about it. We had each been on our feet since Friday morning, shooting twelve-hour days. My greatest memory comes from the drive home from the third wedding. As I slowly drove down Highway 41 to our home ten miles away, the streetlights felt like they were falling in front of me. It happened at least three times before I opened my window to get cold, fresh air into the car. Minutes later, a streetlight started coming down again. I pulled over in exhausted paranoia. Taking a quick snooze in a parking lot five minutes from our house, I woke up realizing that the streetlights weren't falling—my eyelids closing just made it appear like they were.

Everyone we knew—everyone—said we were crazy. "You have to be able to live," we were told. A few of our family members saw the progress we were making along the way and began to understand more. But for the most part, we were those "crazy people following some nut who wrote a book." That wasn't paraphrasing—that was from someone close to us at the time.

Baby Makes Four...

Late in the evening on September 19th, Elizabeth's breathing made it obvious that our lives were about to change once again. Nine months pregnant with our second child, she was admitted to the hospital, and our Nolan was born late the next morning with no problems—if you don't count me passing out onto the hospital floor while holding my wife's hands during the epidural. Our adorable little blond baby was born on a Thursday, which, in the middle of wedding season, was another blessing. Any wedding photographer who is an expectant dad has a big worry about their wife going into labor on a wedding day.

After two exhilarating, exhausting days, Nolan was discharged from the hospital on Saturday. The wedding I was to photograph was the same day. I was fortunate that he came home early, but I was hoping it would be on Friday or Sunday.

Our friend, Justin, who lived just a few blocks away, drove Elizabeth and Nolan home from the hospital and was happy to check on them during the day. Meanwhile, I photographed the preparation and ceremony, and with the hospital only a few minutes away, I tried to get there before they left. I didn't make it to the hospital, but I made it to CVS, where they parked so Elizabeth could get her medicine. I gave our little guy in the backseat a kiss before heading to the reception.

The reception was a blast, but I couldn't wait to get home and see Nolan. I scooted to the bar to grab a glass of water when a friend who was a wedding guest greeted me with an icy blast of sarcasm.

"Sucks that you have to do this," he said with more than a hint of pity.

I assumed he was talking about working instead of being with my son, but he mentioned how I had to photograph weddings on the weekends while working my job during the week.

I smiled, knowing we were less than six months from quitting our day jobs and becoming free to run our business—and our lives—the way we dreamed of. For months, he told me about how much he hated his job and wanted to get out, but he saw no way to do so. In his mind, the only option was to stay where he was. He partied on the weekends, and then faced the dreaded Monday morning commute.

I saw him months later, after we quit our day jobs. His situation was no different than it was during that wedding reception. Actually, it had grown worse. He still saw no way out. Enthused by what we had learned, I attempted to steer him toward starting his own business. He's a smart guy with great ideas. Yet, it was met with resistance. And when there wasn't resistance, there were excuses. Begrudgingly, I said to myself what he had said to me months earlier.

"Sucks that you have to do this."

One of the most difficult and disappointing aspects of this journey was learning how to ignore the naysayers who discouraged us from trying to get our financial life in order. We knew what we were doing was going to lead to a better life. We could see multiple benefits throughout our lifetime together from just a few years of deep sacrifice. But being in debt has become so normal and so universally accepted that you are considered weird if you go against it.

So, let us be weird.

Delaying Gratification

One of the lessons we learned was the power of delayed gratification. Everything is so easy to buy, and so quickly, that there is hardly a reason to even practice delayed gratification. Credit cards, lightning-fast internet, and businesses built around getting you information and products in no time have assured this.

I've always been wired toward delaying gratification. As a kid, my grandparents would bring over a box of Dunkin' Donuts each time they visited. I loved those donuts, especially the ones with the raspberry filling. Each time I ate one of those delicious balls of dough, I noticed all the jelly was squeezed into one end. The other side was pure dough. The worst thing for me would be to bite into the donut jelly first and be left with nothing but sugared dough. So, I devised a plan. I'd see where the jelly was inserted and make a calculated decision on where the bulk of the jelly was placed. I would then surgically munch away at the dough until I got to the deep red, gooey jelly heaven that finished off my donut experience.

While I was messing around with donuts in the late '70s, Walter Mischel was in the middle of a long-term experiment with marshmallows at Stanford University's Bing Nursery School. Mischel, along with his graduate students, gave the young students a choice: eat one marshmallow immediately, or waited twenty minutes and get two marshmallows to eat.

Mischel followed up on these children as they grew into adults, and the results are astonishing. The study showed that the child's ability to delay eating the first marshmallow predicted a lower body mass index and higher SAT scores thirty years later. In a related, but separate study of the same children, the parents of the children able to resist the temptation of the first marshmallow were more competent than the children who weren't—and this was without the parent even knowing if their child ate the first marshmallow or waited for two.

As you can see, delaying gratification is a huge advantage.

'The Year of Work' beat us up as much as it propelled us. It taught us lessons and knocked us down. It pushed our limits and extended our resilience. It tested all our principles and established new ones. It made us question so many of our previous beliefs. If we were a diamond, that was the year all the pressure created a gem. It was, without a doubt, the most difficult, challenging, and eventually, most rewarding year during the entire process.

With a toddler, a newborn baby, a growing business, and a full-time job, this was the point where the rubber met the road. As the year wound down, we finished with a flurry, like a marathon runner gaining speed in the final mile. We had four weddings scheduled in December, which is typically a slow month for nuptials.

We clawed, scraped, and negotiated for whatever work we could get during the "offseason" to speed up our plan.

As the new year approached, we could finally see light at the end of the tunnel. We had paid down our mortgage to just under $30,000. Barring any catastrophic issues, we couldn't envision a scenario where we wouldn't be completely debt free sometime the next year. We didn't know it then, but the hardest work was complete. Maybe it's because we were so tired. Maybe it's because we worked so intensely that it took time to process.

We enjoyed a quiet New Year's Eve celebration with our new family of four, and even managed to make it all the way to midnight. After we put the kids to bed, Elizabeth and I enjoyed a quiet moment with a glass of Champagne, finally giving ourselves a few minutes to reflect on the watershed year we had just voluntarily put ourselves through.

"So," I said to my lovely wife before we got ready for bed, "would you do one more year like that?"

She looked at me with a combination of exhaustion and outright steely determination.

"Are you crazy?" she asked matter-of-factly. She was asleep minutes later. She had a point. I was crazy.

But would you trade a year of exhaustion for a lifetime of freedom?

New Year, New Life

On New Year's Day, where it seems so many of our big decisions have been made, we finally crafted our exit plan from full-time employment. I once heard a line about business that has stuck in my head ever since: When your full-time job starts getting in the way of your side business, it's time to leave your full-time job. That is exactly where we stood on that chilly, January morning.

Like I mentioned earlier, the one professional aspect of leaving my job at the newspaper I fretted over was my losing the assignments photographing professional sports. From the start of my photography journey in 1994, I shot in as many stadiums as possible. Once I started shooting games, I made the audacious goal of trying to get credentialed in every professional sports venue in the United States.

As of that January, I had photographed in nearly sixty venues, but had more than eighty to go, with new ones always being built.

I was photographing the Indianapolis Colts, as I did often, through their playoff run. They hosted the Chargers, and I was on the sidelines once again. This time felt different, though. I knew that this might be the last NFL game I would shoot for a long time. Possibly ever. If the Colts won, I would get at least one more game and a chance to photograph the Super Bowl. But as the Chargers rallied to eliminate the Colts, I tried to take it all in. I took my time walking back to the photo workroom. It was such a joy and privilege to do this for all those years, but I was voluntarily walking away from it. Taking in the sights, smells, and the feel of the building, I walked out to the field one last time like an athlete about to retire. That was the one afternoon I regretted the decision to leave my job.

What caused me more angst was shutting down the goal to photograph in all the venues. I eventually wanted to turn the project into a book. Everyone I mentioned it to thought it was an incredibly cool idea. But without a newspaper to work for, and the press credentials that come with it, the project would be left to die. Or at best, put on pause. But my personal project would be getting in the way of our family progress. I finished up that evening and slowly headed for the elevator leading me out of my previous life.

We had more than twenty-five weddings booked for 2008, and the potential for possibly ten more. Financially, we were at the point where we could live off our business alone. We still had the mortgage, which we were gung-ho on knocking out that year, but it was no longer the reason why we couldn't quit and go on our own. We had built up a cash reserve in the bank to handle any unforeseen financial problems. All that was left for us to do was pull the trigger.

We looked at the calendar and bounced back and forth between different dates. Our wedding season didn't kick in until March, so there was no reason to rush our decision. After a slightly gleeful conversation, almost like deciding what you wanted on your Christmas list as a kid, we agreed that April 8th would be the day. Seeing it in writing made it seem almost surreal. We were quitting our jobs and striking out on our own.

Bolstered by our decision, I made a trip to the bank that week to drop another $5,000 on the mortgage like an experienced gambler at a table in Vegas. The mortgage was now down below $25,000, which was another milestone in the journey.

Priming the Pump

In Zig Ziglar's book, See You at the Top, he gives the example of priming a pump to get water. He explained that to get the water at the bottom of a well, you need to prime the pump over and over. He would describe the struggle of continually pumping and not receiving anything in return. Pushing and pumping, your arms tire, making it easy to think that nothing will ever come from it. But you keep pumping because you know the water is in there.

Suddenly, a drip comes out. Only a drip? All this pumping and I get one lousy drip? But you still don't quit. A few more drips come out, and even though you know it's not enough for a sip, you feel the momentum of all your struggles for the first time. Filled with resolve and purpose, you find a way to pump harder. Within seconds, a half stream of water emerges, and then—BOOM! —water pours out of the well. Before you know it, it's coming out so fast you need buckets to contain the vast amounts of clear, crisp aqua.

This example was very similar to what we were experiencing. We had buckled up and paid off more than $120,000 in debt, started and grew a new business, had two beautiful little boys, and were starting to see the rewards from all the sacrifice we had taken on. Those nights of not going out to dinner didn't matter. We didn't regret holding out on a new car. All the ridicule, snide jokes, and objections we received meant nothing. We were about to do something all the naysayers could only dream of: we were about to live life on our terms.

The Final Countdown

At work, I began a countdown to self-employment. Each time I entered the second-story stairwell leaving the newsroom, I updated the countdown. "100 days," I said to myself the first day back at work. Each day, I kept track and never lost sight. The last thing we needed was to justify staying in this job any longer than necessary.

There is something about doing the right thing that amazingly makes things swing in the correct direction. In January, we booked three more weddings and put the retainers directly toward the mortgage. We wanted to have that balance as low as possible by the time we quit. Cutting our income and having to pay for our own health insurance and equipment was going to take the margin out of our budget to aggressively pay down the mortgage.

Our wedding season kicked off on March 16th, and we prepared for it like a band prepares for the opening night of a world tour. Purchasing new equipment to replace our rapidly aging gear was the one setback to our mortgage-payment snowball. As January blended into February, Elizabeth and I agreed that we should let our bosses know we were planning on leaving early to give them a head start on finding a replacement.

Nobody was shocked. They all told us that they saw this coming ever since our business started succeeding. Our bosses made it very comfortable for us to cut ties, and they appreciated the advanced warning. There was something about that meeting that made it easier to leave sooner. That time was over. We knew it now.

As the warmer winds of March blew in, we finally said it was time. With no more thought than if we were choosing grilled chicken or a cheeseburger for lunch, Elizabeth and I decided March 14th would be the day. With little fanfare, I walked into my editor's office to relay the news of our imminent departure.

I had quit jobs before. Many times. Many, many times. I've been, uh, "dismissed" from others, as well. But those were all times when I was single and my only responsibility was beer and Cheetos. Since we were married, I have been able to count on a steady paycheck to support us and, eventually, our children. This was now completely different.

Dealing with the Doubters

It seemed like everyone was scared for us but us. A month before we quit, someone close to us was shaken by our decision to become self-employed and grilled us about the future. This well-meaning, worried person couldn't let the issue go and bristled at our enthusiasm. They threw question after question at us but no answer was sufficient.

"What will you do about health insurance?" they asked with a look that said a hidden problem had been found.

"We're going to pay for it," I said with a slightly insulted tone. She looked at me like I had two heads. "You do know that we can pay for our own health insurance, right?" I asked.

She had no idea. That's when I realized the emotional battle we were going to deal with. Having been an employee her entire life, this was so foreign she couldn't even understand it. The conversation continued without me being involved. As if I didn't have enough motivation—like raising our family—to make sure this was going to work, something I overheard from a different room gave me the resolve that hardened me like steel to never allow failure to occur.

"They'll see," another voice declared, assured that we were going to find out the hard way that we were making a mistake.

I was as hurt as I was motivated. It was now inevitable that we would succeed; otherwise they would be proven right. There was now no way we were going to fail.

Freedom

And so it went, until March 14th finally arrived. I checked the balance on our mortgage that morning, and it stood at a tad over $15,000. We were close enough. It was time to go. Our co-workers celebrated with cake and stories, but it felt muted.

Elizabeth was already long gone from the paper, and I packed my last few belongings and exited a deserted newsroom. There was no big goodbye, no farewell greetings, no gold watch. Just a few reporters typing away furiously to get their stories in for deadline. Too many employees had come and gone to make a fuss each time someone else left. I was no exception. After eight years, I felt like the human version of yesterday's newspaper before I exited the building.

The ending was surreal, but after a strange ten-minute drive home, Elizabeth greeted me with a giant smile and a huge hug at the front door.

"Freedom!" she whispered to me as she held baby Nolan in her arms.

At least for us, the first week of self-employment was odd. We shot a wedding the previous Saturday, so we got right on the post-processing for that, but being that we both worked in the business, there were some pretty deep habits to adjust to.

Time, all of a sudden, seemed to be abundant rather than constrained. But with great freedom comes great responsibility.

It was obvious—extremely obvious—that we could get very complacent if we allowed ourselves to. I've never been a guy who likes to follow directions, so it would be more of a struggle for me. Elizabeth is task-oriented and focused. I have a tendency to get lost on rabbit trails.

It took three months for us to establish a semblance of a routine. By that time, we had our financial legs under us again. We hadn't put a dime toward the mortgage since we quit our jobs, but with new work coming in, we were now in position to finally attack this final debt and fully experience freedom. By July, we had the money in the account to pay it off in full. If it wasn't for that enlarged security gland my wife possesses, I would have been at the bank that afternoon knocking out that debt.

Elizabeth was more comfortable doing it in two or three more payments. I wanted to haggle with her, but relented. I made a payment for $5,000, followed two weeks later for a similar amount. Our mortgage was down to four digits. It didn't even look right on the computer screen. We used to owe more than that for furniture. Now we were one payment away from not owing a dime to anybody.

We're Debt Free!

August 7th, 2008, started like any other day. We made breakfast for each other, played some music, and danced in the kitchen with the boys. We took Andrew to preschool, hired a babysitter for a few hours, and drove over to the bank. We slipped into the office of the kind gentleman who actually put our mortgage loan together six years earlier. Ironically, the first question he asked us was if we were looking to open up a credit card. Elizabeth and I turned toward each other with a big smile. She let me do the honors.

"Not exactly," I responded. "We're here to pay off our mortgage."

"Really?" he said, genuinely surprised. "How old are you, if you don't mind me asking?"

"I'm thirty-six," I answered.

"I'm thirty," Elizabeth added.

"Did you win the lottery?" he asked, looking up from our paperwork. We laughed at the question, but he wasn't joking. "I don't remember anyone as young as you two coming in to pay off their mortgage," he told us as we went through the tedious process of finalizing all the paperwork.

And with a couple of signatures, that was it. It was over. We walked out of the bank toward bright blue skies, holding hands, completely debt free.

We celebrated with a hibachi lunch together. I'm not sure what I expected to happen, but whatever it was, it didn't happen. There were no rainbows, fireworks, or balloons. There were no parties or celebrations. We didn't even feel comfortable telling some family and friends to avoid making them feel bad. It felt like any other day, but it wasn't. It was the day we finally felt freedom. After nearly four years of working toward it, it still took a few weeks to sink in.

On January 1st, 2004, we started on the path of becoming debt free, and we successfully completed that enormous challenge on August 7th, 2008. Elizabeth and I worked together to fight off all the influences thrown at us about the normality of being in debt. It seems odd when I think about it, because up until fifteen years ago, nobody would have thought of perpetual debt as normal. Now, when you say the word car, the word payment is usually attached. When you say home, you attach mortgage to it. When you say student, you just assume they have a loan.

It has, unfortunately, been sold to the masses and accepted. You are actually considered weird if you don't have debt. Like it's a bad thing you don't owe money. Isn't that strange? We said no. No more. Not for us. Not for our family. Not for their future. Not for our legacy.

The Long-Awaited Scream

After listening to hundreds upon hundreds of Dave Ramsey listeners call into his show to do their debt-free scream, it was finally our turn. The day after we ended our debt cycle, I placed the call to Dave Ramsey's show for our moment in the sun. Elizabeth worked in our office upstairs, both of our sons took naps, and I waited on hold for fifty minutes. Suddenly, on the radio playing in the other room, Dave kicked off his final segment of the hour.

"On the line we have Vincent and Elizabeth..." Elizabeth came bolting down the stairs to sit next to me. Neither of us had ever been on the radio before, so we were both nervous to talk. I don't even remember the questions he asked, but I remember him calling us weird, in a good way. After telling Dave how we paid off more than $140,000 in less than four years, Elizabeth and I screamed "We're debt free!" while trying not to wake up our boys. He thanked us, we hung up the phone, and the journey was complete.

The Opportunities Freedom Affords

Life, as we knew it, flipped 180 degrees. Instead of dreading getting dressed for work each day, Elizabeth and I awoke each morning with excitement instead of angst. Our bank account grew while the time we had to work decreased. Instead of pinching pennies as we had grown accustomed to, we were free to do what we wanted on a day-to-day basis.

That discipline we were forced to embrace taught us to finally be smart with the money we had coming in. We were not yet millionaires, but many multi-millionaires would have envied the time freedom we enjoyed. Millionaires might enjoy long, relaxed lunches at five-star restaurants or at the country club. We did it at Chick-Fil-A. I'll take the spicy chicken sandwich and a strawberry shake over a country-club lunch anyway, so we didn't feel like we missed much.

Less than five years after our journey out of debt began, we had surpassed the lifestyle we enjoyed before our awakening, now with freedom to control each day.

Should I Just Have Been Happy?

I was trained to believe I was worth less money as an employee than I actually was. Each day on the job increased my experience, knowledge, and connections. I became more valuable each day. But with our meager yearly pay increases, we weren't even keeping up with inflation. Fear and a perceived security kept me in the job longer than I would have chosen.

"You should just be happy to have a job in this economy," a co-worker told me.

For a long time, I believed that. By believing that, I convinced myself I was only worth what they were willing to pay me. By convincing myself I was only worth what they offered me, I had accepted their income as my financial ceiling. Not only that, but if they decided I was no longer worth that amount—or any amount—they could let me go in a heartbeat. If I wasn't building something on the side, I learned, I was in serious danger. Believing that a full-time job is secure is insanity. There are exceptions, of course, like being a tenured university professor, but for the rest of us, we are all one phone call away from being tossed out on our butts.

When I decided to finally quit, that same co-worker could not understand the risk.

"Why aren't you worried about your job security?" she asked. "It's so unpredictable."

What she failed to grasp was that newspaper jobs—any job, really—are unpredictable, too. At least we had more control over it.

After all, our decision to leave wasn't an irrational idea built out of exhaustion or frustration. We spent time building the business on the side. We had gotten the proverbial boat close to the dock so we could transition without much risk of falling into the water. The time we used to spend watching movies were spent on growing the business. It took more than two years of side hustle to get to the point where we could even think about quitting. We had twenty-nine weddings booked at that time and about a dozen corporate shoots and sports assignments. I explained our schedule to her before responding.

"If one person fires me," I explained, "we have all these other clients. One person firing us might equal five percent of our income. And new clients are calling weekly, so even that work can be replaced, often at a higher rate, so I think we'll be fine. But if one person fires you, your income immediately goes to zero. You lose one-hundred percent of your income. What would you do tomorrow?"

From Super Stressed to the Super Bowl

Do you remember the story of the Pittsburgh Steelers making the Super Bowl in 2006 and me deciding not to go even as an available ticket stared me in the face?

Three years later, they were on the cusp of another Super Bowl appearance. They were playing the San Diego Chargers in a divisional playoff game and our boys were decked out in their Steelers gear along with their dad. We watched as the Steelers took apart the Chargers on a snowy Pittsburgh afternoon while advancing to the AFC Championship Game. They were once again one win from the Super Bowl. Only this time it would have even more historical significance. Another championship would give Pittsburgh six Super Bowl trophies, something no other team had accomplished to that point.

We put the kids to bed after the game, and I was back at the bar in the basement. I viewed the laptop screen just like I had three years earlier. Once again, I was researching prices for the Super Bowl. I learned three years earlier that ticket prices can skyrocket once the Super Bowl teams are set, so it was best to look early. If I bought a ticket, the risk was that the Steelers wouldn't make it, and I would need to sell it to make the money back.

I saw her slippers descending the steps. Halfway down, she saw my face illuminated in the blue light of my computer.

"What are you doing?" she sarcastically and playfully asked.

"Uh, nothing," I responded. "Just checking out Super Bowl prices..."

"And?" she questioned.

"There is actually a single seat, good section for... hmmmm... $1,600."

Her eyes widened and she gave me that look. Her look. With no hesitation, Elizabeth put her foot down.

"Buy the ticket," she said matter-of-factly.

"Are you crazy?" I asked. "Just like that? Just buy it?"

"You didn't go last time," she explained. "I've heard you talk about that for three years. This is why we did all that work—so when something like this happens, we can do it. More importantly, I don't want to hear you talk about whether you should buy a ticket for the next two weeks. You are going to drive me crazy! Just buy it now."

So, I did. With taxes and fees, I spent more than $1,800 for one little cardboard ticket for one three-and-a-half-hour game. And it was so worth it.

The Steelers defeated the Arizona Cardinals in one of the greatest games in Super Bowl history. Two plays that will go down in Super Bowl lure—James Harrison returning an interception 100 yards for the longest play in Super Bowl history and Santonio Holmes' toe-tapping catch to win the game with thirty-nine seconds left—occurred the night I was there.

Walking out of the stadium, I told myself that if I would have known how great it was, I would have paid twice as much to be there. To see my favorite team—the team I have rooted for since I was seven—win a world championship in person in the most dramatic way possible was a dream come true.

Being Weird Works

To do it the way we did made it even more special. We sacrificed like crazy. We cut everything. We were like salmon swimming upstream against a culture of debt, and the salmon made it. As I walked out of Raymond James Stadium in Tampa on that chilly Sunday night, I did so not owing any money. It was paid for in cash. Memories, not credit card bills, followed me home.

A few months after the journey ended, Elizabeth and I adjusted to our new life of financial freedom. Surprisingly, we didn't change a lot in terms of spending. We invested more. We traveled more. But we didn't increase our lifestyle much or start buying all sorts of things we felt deprived of during our four years of financial fasting. We just had more time to think about what we really wanted out of life. For our kids, for our family, and for ourselves. We wanted time together. We wanted the ability to work, but if the weather was gorgeous, we wanted to head to the park. We wanted the flexibility to travel last-minute and not worry about how to pay for it, or to ask permission. We wanted life on our terms.

While we were piling up debt, and subsequently digging out of it, there was no time to think. We were rats in the wheel. Money comes in, money goes out—only the names changed. The stress level that debt put on our relationship was unbearable. Our worst arguments always had something to do with money.

Sonya Britt, a Kansas State University researcher, found that couples who argued about money early in relationships, regardless of income, debt, or net worth, were at greater risk for divorce. Her study showed that it wasn't children, sex, or in-laws that were the top predictors of divorce—it was money arguments. She also found that money fights were also longer and more intense than other marital disagreements. The study showed that it takes couples longer to recover from a fight about money than any other type of argument.

We weren't any different. Even today, while our money arguments are at much more diluted level than they used to be, when they do happen, they are more intense than any other disagreement we have. We just had our first money argument in several months—on Valentine's Day, no less—and for a few hours we slipped back into our former lives. What's amazing is that it wasn't anything urgent or imminently harmful in any way to our lives. It was about the size of our emergency fund, a position our 2006 selves would have drooled over. But it was surprising that the argument had the same intensity as when we struggled to save our first $1,000.

The beauty of being financially free is that those types of disagreements are extremely rare. Our goals changed from how much we owe to how much we want to save or give. It changes the entire game. Sending out gifts just because we want to is not only easy but enjoyable. I hate to say it, but it used to be painful. Very painful. It's not easy to help others when you are drowning in debt. I found nothing noble in living that way. It turns out that the best way to help people who are struggling financially is to not be one of them.

The Big Move

Eighteen months after our self-employment began, we settled nicely into our new lifestyle, but after the Christmas holidays ended and our families left our home for theirs, I felt a sense of unease. We had lived in Indiana for eight years and had grown comfortable, but with two little boys, and living so far away from both our families, something didn't feel right. Elizabeth saw it on my face and questioned my uncomfortable silence. I responded bluntly.

"What are we still doing here?"

She confided in me that she had been wondering the same thing. The kids were about to start school. We lived fifteen hours from my family and eight hours from hers. Every day we lived there made it more difficult to eventually leave. We both agreed that once the kids started school, we didn't want to pull them out and move. And we had the freedom of choice.

"Are we fine living here until the kids graduate high school?" Elizabeth asked me.

Neither one of us was happy with that thought. It took no more than a thirty-minute talk to conclude that we could make this business successful in another city. Everything we learned was valid anywhere we lived. It wasn't exclusive to Evansville. With her family in Cleveland, and mine in New York, we quickly decided to choose a place convenient to both cities. Having grown up a Steelers fan, I naturally pushed for Pittsburgh. It turns out that it's hard to get a girl from Cleveland to move to Pittsburgh. I explained that it's a beautiful city, on the rise, with tremendous business upside for us. All we needed to do was find new clients to continue this lifestyle.

We made an impromptu trip to the Steel City, where Elizabeth fell in love with it immediately. The vibrant downtown and the rolling hills of the suburbs drew her in.

And again, on yet another New Year's Day, we made the initial decision to uproot our family. Being that we had a full year of weddings booked in Indiana, and a few for the following year, we weren't in a big rush. We pulled out the calendar and tentatively decided that the move could take place the following July. We had a year and a half to put this thing together. And with the NHL's Winter Classic on television in the background, Elizabeth and I started researching neighborhoods around Pittsburgh.

Our business, at that point four years old, was one of the most successful photography businesses in Evansville. After four years of steady progress, our rates in Indiana were at the top of the market. But we knew nobody in Pittsburgh, and we were going to have to start all over again, though with much higher prices. It was like ripping up the roots of a tree and starting over.

But financial freedom clears the way for uncommon options.

What Would It Feel Like to Be Financially Free?

How would your stress levels change? Would you be more optimistic about your future? What about your kids' futures? Would you be a better spouse if you didn't worry or fight about money? What could you give if you were financially free?

Who could you help that truly needs it? How much can you save for your future? For your travel? For your dream house? How much more time could you spend with your kids? Your spouse? Your friends? How much more could you volunteer if you weren't going to a job you disliked to pay for things you already bought?

Debt robbed us of the ability to live the life we wanted because we were paying for a part of our life we already lived.

Breaking the Chains

Once we no longer had to worry about daily money stress, we were able to focus on doing work we loved, adding value to the lives of others, and investing in our relationships and our health.

Within our photography business, it gave us the ability to hone our craft toward our strengths and passions. That allowed us to have a unique look at an oversaturated industry instead of following trends or dropping prices to compete.

Standing out in any industry naturally allows you to charge more for what you are worth and the flexibility to value your time more. The time we save by not having to funnel extra hours into our business also affords us the opportunity to work on other business opportunities and personal passion projects, such as coaching others who want a similar situation for their lives and my goal to travel the United States photographing the behind-the-scenes world of professional sports in every stadium for my future book *One Shot*.

Most importantly, this schedule allows us the freedom to base all our work ventures around our family life. Assignments, no matter how lucrative, are not scheduled around our children's birthdays, holidays, or important family dates. Having the ability to block off time for extended family vacations, one-on-one trips, and just day-to-day time together gives us the work-life balance we dreamed of from the moment we thought of starting a family. Speaking of time, what could possibly be more valuable? There is no price I can put on an impromptu afternoon wiffle ball game in the back yard. It's calming to not have money dictate our decisions like it used to.

I'm not suggesting that you have to become completely debt free to attain your own freedom, but I am suggesting that being in control of your money is essential to keep your money from controlling of you. But what you must control to attain true freedom is your time.

For us, becoming debt free was an important part of our plan to get to the next level. With each step, a new world opened up. I'll be the first to tell you that this isn't easy. Those four years of reigning in our spending, making ourselves uncomfortable, and working toward a gigantic task shaped who we are today. It showed us that we have the ability to accomplish so much more than we could have imagined for ourselves, but it took difficult situations to prod us into action.

When I was thirty-two, we were broke, in jobs going nowhere, and starting a family. Four years later, we had complete control over our time and money, and were able to retire from "the grind." In just four short years, we turned our life, family, and future completely around.

The greatest gift I received was not getting what I thought I needed. I think back to that crucial meeting with my boss when I was at the newspaper. What if he had offered me a 10% raise instead of a 3% increase? I would have taken it.

We never would have started our business. We would have made just enough money to get by, but not enough to have the courage to quit. I wouldn't have started reading all those books, and my outlook would have remained negative.

I can envision many nights coming home to a tired wife and a baby, complaining about work at the dinner table. I can hear the money fights. I can see the need to earn more once that pay increase was gobbled up, trying to figure out where to find the time to do so. It's easy to see a household riddled with stress as more children were born. It's also easy to see a marriage fractured by that stress. In a world where the number one cause of divorce is money problems, it's not difficult to see that our family would have faced a much darker future.

That raise, or lack of one, was low enough that it forced me to take action. If our story can help any family change course and start building the life and family of their dreams, then all this is worth it. We all deserve the opportunity for a bright future. We all hold the opportunities for freedom in our own hands, regardless of what the news or the naysayers tell us. If you want it, you can do it. If Elizabeth and I were able to, I am positive you can, too.

Henry Ford, the man behind the Ford Motor Company, coined a phrase that stuck with us, and I hope it sticks with you.

"Whether you believe you can or you believe you can't, you are right."

The key to financial success is not your income, it is your intensity. But the key to success in life is your health and your relationships. I can't emphasize this enough. Never lose sight of that.

BONUS MATERIAL

When writing a book, there is never enough space for everything to make it into the physical book. Thanks to the internet, we can fill those gaps! So if you are enjoying this, and want more behind the scenes stories, please visit

thefreelancetribe.com/bonus

It features bonus stories that didn't make the book, including...

- The story behind what pushed me to started writing Freelance to Freedom.
- The career changing story from Lambeau Field in Green Bay about how I got my first NFL press pass.
- How the mafia got me into a baseball game when I was 15, and what it taught me about life.
- The full story about when I was arrested for stealing (mentioned briefly on page 10).
- What happened when I snuck into Giants Stadium and hid inside of a bathroom stall for four hours just to photograph an NFL game.

Come on over to thefreelancetribe.com/bonus to read these and more!

Also, I run a free online community as well as an exclusive membership site. We support, help and coach ambitious freelancers and small business owners to knock out debt, become financially free, and optimize their businesses to give themselves and their families a life of time, money and location freedom! Please join us!

thefreelancetribe.com

PART II

THE FIVE STAGES OF
FREELANCE
TO FREEDOM

P art I was our story. Part II is about you. When we started this journey, we were broke, scared, in debt, and lost. Less than four years later, we built a thriving freelance career, paid off all our debt, and were living our ideal life of freedom. We recently hit a net worth of seven figures, while never making more than $130,000 in a single year until that point, with many of those years in the five figures.

Part II of Freelance to Freedom will show, help, and guide you toward a life of money, time, and mental freedom. Even those who are employees (and look to remain that way) can create a life of freedom much greater than what you currently have. But time freedom is reserved only for those who control their time, and that's impossible to do if someone else controls your schedule.

Here is a breakdown of what we are about to dive into.

Phase I — Escaping the Seeds of Discontent

Phase I, unfortunately, is where a majority of the workforce finds itself. Eighty percent of employees do not like their jobs. They are looking for a way out, but feel stuck. They often have little money saved, are stretched for time, have fallen into an unhealthy lifestyle, and have stress in their home lives.

At the same time, most do have a dream to do something different. Commonly, it is not to find a different full-time job. Instead, they feel drawn to starting a side business doing something they have a passion for. They have a desire to help others in some way. They want better control of their time. They want opportunity to make more money. And they want more time with their kids and their spouse. But they feel stuck, lost, and unsure where to start.

Phase II — The Side Hustle

This is a phase of tremendous growth. It also comes with a lot of pain. If you didn't have a side business already, this is where you start one. It's also where you see so many of the mistakes that you made in the past. You learn the difference between being an entrepreneur and a freelancer, figure out what you actually love doing, and go through tremendous growing pains.

It's where you start to get control of the money you have, shape a plan for the future, and get a glimpse of the life you truly desire. This is the phase where you make your biggest business mistakes and learn your greatest lessons, setting you up for the growth you will see in Phase III.

Phase III — The Optimal Freelancer

In Phase III, things are looking up.

You are bringing in more than 50% of the income you need to live off from your business. You may have already quit your day job, or are close to doing so. You are now paying down your debt with your business income. You've researched all your investment options and have the insurance you need to protect you from danger.

Your family life is also in a better place. You are more attentive to your family. The stress and drama you felt is beginning to fade. You are more energized than anxious. You realize that with money freedom comes mental freedom. With more mental freedom, you start coming up with new ideas, which is when you have the ability to easily shift between freelancer to entrepreneur. This is the stage when your business, time, and money start to fire at an optimal level.

Phase IV — A Life of Freedom

What would it be like to wake up every day and do exactly what you want to do? What would it feel like to not owe anyone else a dime? What would it feel like to have the abundant time to devote to your spouse, children, and friends?

On top of that, you have a healthy lifestyle, free to exercise without trying to find the time and to eat well without trying to find the money. Phase IV is when an unexpected setback is like driving over a pebble when it used to be like driving into a ditch. You don't have to work as much, but you do because you want to grow, help others, and contribute. It makes you feel alive. You can't see the difference between working and playing.

The clients you take on are hand-selected, and you have the financial freedom to turn down the clients who aren't a good fit. With this extra time and money, it's easy to create time for ideas that can bring in passive income, sending you deeper into Phase IV. It's the area where nearly every self-employed person dreams of being, but where very few get.

Phase V— Every Day Is Independence Day

Phase V is simple. Time freedom. Financial freedom. Location freedom. Life freedom. What more could you want?

PHASE I

ESCAPING THE SEEDS OF DISCONTENT

"Discontent is the first step in progress in any man."—Oscar Wilde

The idea for this book, initially, was to share our story about how we started a side business to pay off our debt so we could be successfully self-employed. That's what Part I was about. Through more than a year of writing and many more years of research, it turned out that this idea went much deeper than that.

For us, the idea of being 100% debt free lit the fire under us. For you, it might not. You might crave more time with your family, or you might be inspired to pay off all your consumer debt, but the thought of paying off your house is either too daunting to think about yet, or it's simply not worth the sacrifice. Or you might have the dream to run your own business and escape an unfulfilling job. Everyone's version of freedom is different.

When we went through this, our kids were very young. You might have three kids approaching their teens and don't want to sacrifice those years to debt reduction, yet you still want to achieve greater financial success and time freedom.

That's why we switch gears in Part II. My good friend, Ken Carfagno, who followed these steps while I was writing this book, helped me identify the different stages of self-employment and how to go from stuck, hopeless, and frustrated to free mentally, financially, and with your time.

What is my motivation for writing this?

I'm tired of seeing so many people struggle. I'm frustrated at seeing so many kids coming out of college without even the basic skills for living a free life for themselves. I'm fed up watching so many parents in a stage of utter exhaustion, wondering what happened to their life after believing that following the rules we were all taught would lead them to success rather than the road to nowhere. I'm sad watching so many of us in our thirties and forties miss out on precious time with our families by drowning in meaningless work, and then finding relief inside a bottle of wine. And I want to prevent those about to embark on this journey to learn from our mistakes and successes.

The Dream

Do you have a dream?

Is there something you have always wanted to do with your life that you are not doing now? That thing that you would wake up for without an alarm clock, fired up and ready to go? The thing that you would do for free if you could only afford to? The thing that gives you purpose, helps others, and allows you to live the life you desire? If you are anything like the majority of Americans, your answer is clear.

You have no clue.

You used to have it. We all did. Remember? But somewhere along the way, it was beaten out of us. It was taken away from us as children by well-meaning, dream-stealing adults. It was slowly made to feel impossible by those working under the guise of being "realistic." From rule-following school teachers to concerned parents and jealous classmates, our dreams were collectively crumpled up and tossed into the trash on our way toward the goal of a high school or college diploma.

Instead of being encouraged to create your own life, you were told to get a good job, preferably with benefits. And a matching 401(k) would be nice. It sounded great. It would give you security. But was this how you wanted to spend your life? Was it your dream to be awoken by an alarm clock? When you were younger and excited about your future, did fighting for a spot on a train full of zombies from The Walking Dead thrill you? Or sitting in traffic, day after day? Did spending the prime years of your life working for somebody else doing something you didn't want to do making someone else wealthy for a paycheck that was already spent sound like something you would have signed up for? Did getting home too late to spend time with your kids, night after night, sound appealing?

A Deloitte's Shift Index survey reported that more than 80% of Americans are unhappy in their jobs. That's not the American Dream, it's the American Nightmare.

Our nation's 16th President, Abraham Lincoln, would be distraught by what has happened. In his speech to the Wisconsin Agricultural Association on September 30th, 1859, he laid out clearly what we recognize as the American Dream.

Lincoln told the group that having an independent livelihood was at the center of the American Dream. That the only reason to work for someone else was to get your feet under you, figure out what people needed, and then go set up shop for yourself. He wanted you to create a life of personal sovereignty, liberty, and unmatched freedom. It was almost insulting to work for someone else for an extended period of time.

That was a mere century and a half ago, and boy, have things changed. Those changes explain the dissatisfaction, unhappiness, and overall discontentment in the American workforce.

To all of us alive today, public school feels like it has always been a part of the culture and childhood. In reality, it's a fairly recent addition to our lives. Mass public schooling didn't begin until the 1880's, only 90 years before the first time I started school. Those first students in Massachusetts were forced to attend school by the militia against their parents' pleas. Prior to that, public schooling did not exist. And those times were overflowing with innovation. George Eastman, Nikola Tesla,

Thomas Edison, George Washington Carver, Alexander Graham Bell, and George Westinghouse—just to name a few—came from a time with no public schools. And it was one of the most inventive, creative, explosive eras for growth and prosperity this nation has ever seen.

This is not meant to romanticize the 1800's. That era was plagued by slavery, disease, poverty, and war. I can't imagine any of us would trade the lives we have today for the lives of people back then. Which makes it even more remarkable that so many world-changing inventions came out of that time. The lack of resources was not a match for the free thinking, entrepreneurial mindsets that got this country moving. Looking at where we are today, there is a need to ask what has gone wrong. With all the technology advancements, comfort, and connections, why are we not thriving as a nation?

Not only do we need to learn how to master our money, we need to get back to working for ourselves doing work that has purpose and meaning. Not only do we need to, it's the direction the workforce is headed.

It is projected that in less than ten years, fifty percent of the workforce will be freelancers and the self-employed.

Get Busy Living

I, too, had lost my dream. What I thought was a stable career led me into a nightmare. I was so blinded by what I thought I should do that I failed to see that my job was no longer what I thought it was.

Budget cuts, irregular hours, complaining. I was mentally stuck and headed nowhere good. I returned home each night complaining to Elizabeth at the dinner table. Even though I was performing well, I dreaded going in each day. I secretly wished I would be fired since I didn't have the guts to quit.

Why was I scared to quit? I almost forgot that I never wanted a "job" to begin with. I always wanted to be self-employed. To not answer to a boss. So, how did I wind up there? Somewhere along the way, I unconsciously started chasing someone else's dream.

I never wanted to trade my independence for money. I wanted to have a family where we enjoyed life to the fullest, not to be stressed and stretched for time and money. I never enjoyed following someone else's schedule in school, so why did I want that now?

Simple. To get a job, steady pay, benefits.

I fell into the security trap.

I was less than two months into that job when I started feeling twinges of regret. I was now beholden to someone else's agenda. It took me much longer to confront that feeling.

I realized years later that I no longer could live that life, though it took starting a family to shake me into action. I wanted freedom. Freedom with our money and time. Freedom with our choices and goals. Freedom to decide what I would do each and every day. Freedom to do the work I wanted to do—to determine what to charge, with the right to turn down the work of crazy clients.

The freedom to take vacations without fear of rejection because someone else had already requested that time off.

We've now achieved a level of personal success I couldn't imagine back when I was digging my hand beneath my ripped car seat looking for spare change to buy a cheeseburger. What you are about to read are the lessons, stories, and laws we were taught either through the school of hard knocks or the mentors we followed to help you go live a life of freedom. What was most astonishing to me was that most of the laws of success we learned were shunned by the majority of my peers. If we would have listened to those same voices, we would still be broke, desperate, deflated, and completely normal. Not much different than where we were when this story began. I desperately do not want that for you and your family.

Are you finally ready to take control of your life? Unearth your buried dreams? Create your ultimate life? Time is not slowing down. There are no do-overs. In the words of Red from The Shawshank Redemption, "Get busy living, or get busy dying."

The 18-35 Trap

It's become so common that it's now predictable. That eighteen-year-old college student had it all in front of him. Leaving for school, the future was his. And he did it all right. He followed the rules. He stayed in line. He studied hard for the good grades in high school to get accepted into that coveted university. He chose the promising major, and even though it had a heavy debt attached, it all felt worth it. It was an investment in his future.

And then he wakes up, seemingly overnight, at thirty-five. Only now, he's married, with two kids and a third on the way. They have a nice house with a hefty mortgage. That's what you do when you have a growing family. They are still paying student loans for himself and his wife, who left her position to be home with the kiddos. He was taught that those were 'good debts'. Now the car payments, the mortgage, the student loans, and the credit-card debt are all paid for with his salary. The salary from the job he has grown to despise.

Sunday nights are the worst. That's when his brief reprieve, called the weekend, comes to an end. He feels it in the pit of his stomach as he gets the kids ready for bed. Another week starts with the early morning commute. Some days he drives, stuck in traffic listening to the goofy morning shows. Other mornings, he rides the train packed next to sleepy riders who barely look alive.

"How did this happen?" he asks himself. "How did this become my life?"

The reason he does all of this—his family—he barely gets to see anymore. And when he does, he's exhausted. He coaches his son's team, which is the highlight of his week, but it's the only time they get together anymore, aside from evening tuck-ins and rare vacations. His three-year-old daughter cherishes every moment with her dad, even if it's usually rushed and in passing.

Adding to the stress is the chilly relationship with his wife. They used to have so much fun together, until money issues, time stress, and lack of sleep drove a wedge between the once vibrant couple. It feels like the only time they are alone together is when they wind down in front of the television late at night, passing out next to a glass of wine during the shows they are trying to catch up on Netflix.

Slouching down while riding the train into work, he thinks back to all the big dreams he once had. There was that business he always wanted to try. Those extended family trips they were going to take. That's all faded away now. He can't even allow himself to think about how miserable he is at work because they are barely getting by as it is. Barely getting by, but they make good money. He fails to see the irony. He fears getting laid off, with budget cuts and his bosses noticing his reduced production. With a lack of job satisfaction comes a lack of innovation.

He feels stuck and depressed. He knows that he has to get out, but he doesn't want to take a lateral full-time position. His smile only appears when he thinks of his kids and of starting that business he always dreamed about.

If he doesn't get out of this trap, and soon, he fears he never will.

Were We Educated or Were We Schooled?

But what if that eighteen-year-old didn't follow the cheese into the trap? What if he said no to the debt, job security, and lifestyle indoctrination?

"But they need an education!"

I agree. Children do need an education. But they don't need to get schooled. Who said that an education has to take place inside a university classroom? Some of the smartest, wisest, most successful people I know openly question whether the university plan is wise any longer.

"But without a degree, they can't get a job!"

If you want to be an attorney, doctor, or highly specialized professional, you are correct. But for everyone else, is it absolutely essential any longer?

I am not saying that college is a bad thing. I am neither a doctor nor a lawyer, and I got a tremendous benefit from my time at Ohio University. It was an enlightening, fantastic experience which I have incredibly fond memories of. But those memories would feel different if I walked away from commencement with a $150,000 bill attached to my cap and gown and diminished job opportunities.

Those memories feel great because my degree was largely paid for before graduation. I saved before and worked throughout my time at school, and walked out with less than $10,000 from one student loan. In full disclosure, my parents generously paid that loan as a graduation present.

So, what about that eighteen-year-old today?

What if that teenager didn't sign that application and loan papers? The ones which might come with a $150,000 price tag for everything included, while also missing out on four years of real-world experience. Instead, this teenager starts a small business.

With no debt and a plan, this young adult slowly builds his future empire. He commits to save ten percent of his income into investments like a Roth IRA and a SEP. He also saves ten percent toward the down payment on a future home. He lives on the rest.

Fast forward four years. This twenty-two-year-old weathered a slow and rocky first few years, but managed to expand his business through hard work and relationship building. He now has enough money for a down payment on a house, a retirement account that will grow to more than one million dollars by retirement without adding another penny, and a business that is growing and expanding.

His high-school classmate, the one with the expensive and fancy degree, has more than $100,000 in loans to pay back. This recent graduate has also been trained to go into debt for a job and a lifestyle, and the job force he will be staring at is much tougher than even a few years ago. The future is built for the self-employed, not the employee.

Our young business owner, on the other hand, has already gotten four years of real-world experience. He has learned the tax benefits of the self-employed that our college graduate was never taught. He was never sold on debt. If this bright young person attacked his mortgage right from the start, there won't be a problem paying it off in four years, just like we did. At the same pace, this person will have a paid-off house and a stocked investment portfolio by the age of twenty-five.

Our college graduate, if he follows the regular pattern, leaves school with massive student loans, a more expensive lifestyle, and decent paying job—if they are one of the lucky ones to get a good job. Four years later, if we go by the standard, his student loans haven't been dented, but he now has a car payment and credit-card debt added to the balance sheet.

Now you tell me: who got the education, and who got schooled?

Imagine

The college-graduate route has been sold to us for the past few decades. And why were we taught to get a university degree? So we could get a good job, right? Well, guess what?

Companies like Google, Facebook, Ernst & Young, Penguin/Random House Publishers, Whole Foods, Apple, Starbucks, and Nordstrom no longer require a college degree for employment. And the list is growing every day. So, the bottom is dropping out on that theory in so many ways. That approach is dying, and we collectively need to create a different way.

Can you imagine a world where our twenty-five-year-olds have no debt? Not even "good debt". No student loans. No car payments. No credit-card bills. A world where they are already saving money for their future.

Imagine a world where they owned their own home outright. Where there weren't mortgages, second mortgages, and home equity loans sucking the life out of their incomes. A world where they weren't taught to trade a large mortgage payment for a measly tax deduction. Imagine a world where they didn't rely on someone else for employment. Where they didn't slog into work daily to make someone else wealthy while making themselves sick.

Imagine a world where they build successful businesses doing something that inspired them and benefited others. A business without the burden of debt and the stress that tags along. A world where they are in control of their money, instead of their money controlling them.

Imagine that world.

How much less would we ring our hands about who will be elected next? If we collectively didn't need their promises of better jobs—because we created those jobs—their power would diminish. Taxes would decrease. Healthcare costs would decrease, as well, because, as a society, we would be healthier. Less trips to the doctor means lower costs for everyone. Less stress means less alcohol and drug abuse. Less alcohol and drug use means less crime.

Imagine these twenty-five-year-olds growing older and not stressing about money often. What would their relationships with their children look like? I imagine that it is an infinitely brighter future than if their parents were tired, stressed, unhealthy, and deeply in debt.

How much better would their children's lives be? How much better, and happier would their entire families be? How much more time would they have together to create wonderful memories? How much better would that make their neighborhoods, other local businesses, and the large cities that surround those neighborhoods? How much more could be given to the improvement of these areas? How much better would that make our nation and our world?

Can you imagine?

What Don't I Know?

Have you ever been so sure you were 100% correct about something, only to find out later you were entirely off-base? My friend, John Craig, taught me that the people who believe they are 100% correct on any subject—whether it be politics, business, sports, you name it—are the most dangerous. I've been that person many times, and often I've come to learn that my worldview was as limited as my mental flexibility. I cringe to think of all the times I vehemently argued a point, only to later realize I was wrong. Worse yet, all those times I never realized I was wrong.

A memorable one came during my junior year of high school after a disagreement with my algebra teacher. The details of the argument remain fuzzy, aside from her final words as I walked angrily out the door.

"Vince, you don't know everything!" she snapped, calmer than she probably could have.

Those words bounced around my head as I walked home. With each intersection I crossed, I grew more and more upset. I started repeating those words out loud as I walked across the railroad tracks and through the hole in the fence on my way home. As I approached a few parked cars to my right and walked alongside a blue sedan, I caught my reflection in the car's rear window. Taking a gander at my hat on backwards and my irritated, acne-covered face, I stopped to have a brief, impromptu conversation with my reflected alter ego.

"I don't know everything," I said to myself, offended that she said such a preposterous statement.

Pausing for a moment, I responded to my reflection in the window.

"What don't I know?" I said out loud with an air of complete self-affirmation.

In my mind, I was 100% right. What didn't I know? I was working and making a decent chunk of change for a sixteen-year-old. I had a cute girlfriend. I had a fun group of friends. Sure, my grades were terrible, but I didn't care about that anyway. What more was there? In my life, I believed I had all the answers. Anyone with half a brain who was not inside my skin would immediately see how foolish my thoughts were, but I was convinced I was right.

My mindset was dangerous. When we are convinced we are 100% correct, there is no room for growth. We become stagnant. And stagnation, by definition, means having stopped, or ceasing to run or flow. Stagnation at any age is harmful.

If you are not where you want to be, there is a high probability you have grown stagnant in one or more areas. It's likely you are convinced that what you are doing is absolutely right, even though it's leading to harmful results. It's astonishing to meet so many people that struggle to get themselves to a better place, but refuse to change what got them there in the first place.

Andy Andrews, one of my favorite authors, says a line that I love. It's a line I've had to use on myself many times, even with that teenage meltdown of mine.

"You can't always believe everything you think," Andrews declares.

Believing that you are absolutely, positively 100% correct in any area of life truly comes down to laziness. It proves that we have thought about an issue until we came to a conclusion that fit our mind perfectly well, and then left it alone to stagnate. For example, think about the last time you heard two people arguing about politics. Both of them thought they were 100% correct.

Their minds will not be changed by the conversation. Never mind that they could both be wrong. Never mind that they both probably are wrong, at least a few times into the conversation.

Are you looking to change your life, but are convinced that there is nothing you can do? You are sure you're right. But what if you're actually wrong? What if there is something you don't know yet that not only makes you look foolish, but would make you change your mind, as well? Practice doing this with anything you are positively, 100% sure of. The world is filled with lost souls who are convinced they are right.

Do you believe your job will always be there for you? Do you believe the company you work for has the best interest of your family in mind as much as you do? Are you convinced that a degree is the path to success? Do you see those stories on the news about layoffs and downsizing and believe it cannot happen to you? Do you believe that you will always be in debt?

More importantly, do you believe that you don't have any other options? That this is the best you will ever do and the most money you could ever make? Do you believe that it's too late for you to start something different? Do you think it's impossible to make more money, have more time, and live a better life?

Remember, you can't always believe everything you think.

The Best Time to Plant a Tree

The idea that a full-time job is secure is dangerous thinking in this age of the digital, global upheaval of the workforce. The steady paycheck lulls us into a false sense of security. But when the rug gets pulled out from underneath us, the faithful, hard-working employee is the one left behind.

The best time to plant a tree, the old saying goes, was twenty years ago. The second-best time is today.

The best time to start a side business goes by the same idea. Start one before you need it. When you need the shade from that tree, you will not get it the day it is planted. When you need the income from a side business, you will not get it the day you start. If you wait until you are fired or quit in frustration, you are already behind the proverbial eight ball.

Even if it's one tiny step per day, get started now. When you get started before you need it, you get to decide exactly what to do and how to do it. You won't be pulled by the need to make immediate income from it. It can start as a passion project, a labor of love from something you have done in the past as a hobby or a desire, not a need. Most people view work as a need, something that has to be done in order to have a day or two off to do what they want.

But what if you got to do what you wanted every day? That will happen if you start before you need it.

But I'll Need to Make More Money

Eventually, the goal might be to turn this side business into something to replace your full-time job. I know what you're thinking: there is no way you can turn a hobby or a passion into something that replaces your income.

But how much money do you really need to make? Does a number jump into your head? Say that number out loud. Got it? Okay, I'll bet you a donut and a coffee you are mistaken. I'd be willing to part with a jelly glazed and a large vanilla latte when I tell you that it's probably half the number you mentioned.

I've noticed this trend when I coach small business owners. They were already overwhelmed because they felt the need to increase their income. They started a side business, but it wasn't growing fast enough. They didn't have the time to commit to the work, and they weren't making their work stand out. It was affecting their personal lives, their sleep, and their mood.

I'd ask them how much they needed to make. It was interesting how many people would throw out a round number immediately. Within one month, I had four separate clients bluntly tell me that they each needed $125,000 for their household to make it. After the fourth person told me the same story, I did a few minutes of basic math, and armed with a set of simple questions, took a different approach at the next meeting. I asked again how much they needed, and again they all gave me the same, set number.

Pulling out a yellow pad, I went all accountant on them. I asked how much their food bills were. I asked about utilities. Housing. Insurances. Gas. Taxes. Car. Basic entertainment. Clothes. We tallied up the numbers with each client, all on different days in different locations. And each time, the results were laughably similar. They each needed half of what they were convinced they "needed". I became used to the confused looks on their faces because I had seen it so often.

"Is there anything else you can think of that you need?"

Silence. Eventually, one or two things, like a kid's activity, would creep in, but it was never more than a thousand dollars.

"Are you positive you need $125,000 to get by?" I'd ask. This time, they weren't so sure.

"This doesn't make any sense," one client told me. "We make more than $125,000, and we are just getting by. Where is this money going?"

This practice, for them, was the first step in getting on the right financial path. Their problem was that they believed what they thought. They had increased their lifestyle to fit their income. As their budget got bloated, those wants blended into what they thought were needs. Once we touched on what they needed, they started noticing areas that were bloated, as well. In the end, their new 'need' budget of $70,000 was closer to $60,000.

"Tell me why you need to make more money," I said. "You are already stressed about not having time with your family. You just grabbed your belly and said you haven't exercised in forever, and that you aren't eating well because you are so stressed. Your sleep is awful. The way you're going, if you find a way to make more money, you will just spend it on another made-up need, and you'll have even less time for things that matter.

"Just imagine, if instead of taking on more work, you took on your money," I asked. "This is hard, because we have gotten used to needing what we want. But if you cut your budget from $125,000 to $75,000, you just gave yourself a $50,000 raise. You actually could start working less! Or raise your prices, work less time, and make the same money."

"I need a coffee," he said to me, walking up to the barista at Starbucks and returning with a glorious-smelling caramel-spiced latte and a mouthwatering blueberry scone.

"Where do I start?" he asked while running his fingers through his hair.

"Let's begin with defining what a need is," I said with a smile while holding up his receipt.

One year later, he and his wife had paid off all their consumer debt and increased their business rates. They worked less and made more, which gave them more time with their two toddlers. They had become, as my friend John likes to say, 'Purposefully Poor.' They chose a simpler lifestyle to get what they really wanted for their family while using the hours they saved toward growing their side business. It's the perfect combination.

The Secret to Achieving Financial Freedom

What is the secret to attaining this elusive freedom that we all hear about? It's the question everyone asks.

And if you have made it this far, you already know the secret. The secret is not just how much money you make. The secret is how much you spend compared to the money you earn. You do not need vast wealth to have financial and time freedom. But financial and time freedom will bring extraordinary wealth if you follow this secret.

The secret is to be able to live on as little as possible. The less you need to live on, and the less time you need to give up to make that income, the more freedom you have. By eliminating all our debts, as a family of five, we are able to live off of roughly $35,000 a year. Since becoming self-employed, we haven't had to do that, but knowing we can is the key. Knowing that allows us to think long-term and work on ideas that create multiples streams of income without the need for immediate reward.

The ability to live off $35,000 while being in control of our time is our unfair advantage. We have had years in the past where we've made $75,000 while enjoying multiple extended vacations and few money concerns, but most of all, we enjoyed our time freedom. That freedom gives us the opportunity to do the type of work that allows us to multiply our income when the right opportunity appears.

Discover Your Fruit

Not everyone desires to be wealthy, but everyone wants to have no financial worries. If you can understand the difference, you are on your way. Whenever someone seeks my guidance on getting out of the 'trap', I have them gather up their 'fruit'. Fruit represents the basic expenses of a household.

FRUIT

F- Food
R- Residence
U- Utilities
I- Insurance
T- Transportation

Add all those up. What is that total for you?

Your FRUIT are your necessities. You can add in some entertainment, as well—just don't go crazy. Everything else is a bonus, meaning expendable. If you can be sold on this idea, and live it, you are on your way towards financial freedom.

Could You Live on a Dollar a Day?

If you question whether you can make it on less, use Tesla and SpaceX CEO Elon Musk as your inspiration.

You might be asking, "You want me to look to a guy worth twelve billion dollars for inspiration on how to live on less?"

Before he was a multi-billionaire, Musk was a student at Queen's University in Ontario, Canada. During his first two years at that school, Musk had a fascination with how he could use space exploration, the internet, and energy efficiency to shape the future of humanity.

Musk knew he wanted to move to the United States, so he envisioned what it would be like as a twenty-something in the States trying to start his own technology business while not accepting a job. Getting a job would derail his big plans.

He determined that in the United States, it wouldn't take much to stay alive. A cheap apartment, a computer, and some food (mainly oranges and hot dogs). So, he set a budget of $30 per month to live on. A dollar a day. Food-wise, he figured if he could live on a dollar a day, it would be pretty easy to earn $30 a month.

With the assurance that he did not need a loftier salary to survive, he was now free to pursue the enormous goals he set for himself.

Instead of accepting the American "normal" of taking a job and an increased lifestyle, Musk went a different route by figuring out how little money he could live on and shaped his life from there. Twelve billion dollars later, Musk can afford all the hot dogs and oranges on the planet while he funds space travel to Mars.

The Dollar That Matters Most...

...is the first dollar you make in your business. Why do you think all those barbershops and diners have their first earned dollar bill taped to the wall? It's because it's a big deal!

Obviously, it's not about the size of the sale. If it was, that money would have been used for bigger reasons than being a wall ornament. The importance is the significance of that bill. That green, rectangular piece of currency proves that you started something. It shows that you had guts, perseverance, and the will to push through all the excuses, fears, and doubts. When you factor in the time and effort involved, it might be the hardest dollar you'll ever make in your life.

And it is worth more than all the others for those same reasons.

If you haven't already, find what it takes to go make that first dollar in your business. It will be the one that matters most.

Unrealistic Expectations

During the start of our first business, I developed some unrealistic expectations. One of the first happened when we took out an ad in the newspaper for our services. Does anyone remember a newspaper?

Elizabeth and I spent weeks crafting, perfecting, and designing this artistic masterpiece. The fonts, text, and wording were finally together in the perfect form. The ad would be prominent in the popular wedding page that ran on Wednesdays. I was sure this ad would be the one that jump-started our business.

My sister-in-law, Trish, was in town to meet our new baby. The newspaper arrived that morning, and I rushed to make sure the ad looked perfect. And it looked better than perfect. It stood out like the crown jewel of the page. There was no doubt the phone was ready to ring off the hook.

I raced to the living room, literally to make sure the phone was connected. I found Trish on the phone, talking to my mother-in-law. She was gushing about Andrew, and how cute he was. I stood by anxiously. As she relaxed and enjoyed a long, leisurely conversation, all I could think about was all the business opportunities we were missing.

The ad was in the paper! Doesn't she realize? Any moment, a big-time inquiry could come in, and we were missing it! Her call must have lasted six hours. Or maybe it was twenty minutes. It just felt like six hours. Trish finally hung up the phone. I was relieved that now we could get on with business, even if we missed a few calls.

We wound up receiving a grand total of zero calls that day from the ad. I was still stubbornly convinced that someone called while the phone was tied up. Three months later, we ended the ad campaign. In ninety-one days, we received exactly one phone call from the ad. And we never heard back from them after that initial call.

I learned a quick and embarrassing lesson on unrealistic expectations. Success is a grind. It is a daily practice. When we hear these stories about that one magic bullet that catapulted a business to stardom, there is a reason why they make the news.

It's because they are ridiculously uncommon.

Ideas That Don't Go Away

We all have ideas that will not go away. For me, this book was one. I've had the title for this book in my head for four years, but I was too afraid to start writing it. I was afraid of the rejection.

I was afraid of the critics—or silence. I was afraid of the work taking me and my mind away from my family. It was much easier to keep doing what I was already doing.

But it never went away. Even though I wasn't writing the book, I was always jotting down notes that applied to *Freelance to Freedom*. When I read a book or listened to a podcast, I'd do the same. In the middle of the night, I would wake from a deep sleep to write down an idea, only to find myself unable to fall back to sleep because I was so excited about it.

I started a blog a few years ago, writing stories that were related to the book idea. I found myself with pages upon pages of notes, dozens of stories written, and more ideas than I knew what to do with, but it wasn't until Elizabeth gave me a nice kick in the butt that I actually began the formal process of writing this book. I've been writing for six months now, and have wanted to quit numerous times. I doubted myself. I doubted the content. I doubted why anyone would read it. But I always came back to it.

If an idea keeps coming back to you, it must be something worth doing. If you are unsure what your next step is, think of those ideas you have that will not go away. You never know where it will take you until you start. And then, just as important, finish it.

So, what is your idea that will not go away? What is that thing you would do for free simply because you love it? What is that thing you start on, and four hours later feel like time just shot by? That thing that makes you smile when you talk without even realizing it? If you are at the very beginning of this journey and don't know where to start, start there. It doesn't matter if you think it's valuable. We'll get into that next.

So, what is your idea that will not go away?

Acres of Diamonds

Russell Conwell, an accomplished lawyer, newspaper editor and clergyman, raised more than seven million dollars to start Temple University in 1887. And he raised the money by giving more than 6000 lectures where he told the story call 'Acres of Diamonds'.

The intriguing story is about Al Hafed, a wealthy man who owned a farm with grain fields, gardens and Orchids. One night, Hafed's friend told him a story about the value of diamonds, and how he could purchase an entire country with a few diamonds and a mine of diamonds could provide lifetime wealth for his children.

This wealthy man woke the next morning feeling poor. Hafed sold his farm, left his family with neighbors and set out on a quest to find diamonds.

Not even knowing what diamonds in their raw form looked like, he set off on a journey for his future fortune. The man went to Palestine and Europe, and while running out of money, arrived in Spain. After multiple failures and endless frustration, he threw himself into the ocean and drowned.

Back at the farm he sold, the man who bought the land found an interesting stone which he brought inside his home to display. Not long after, a friend asked where he found that stone. The farm owner replied that he found it in the tiny creek along his property. He thought it looked interesting, so he brought it inside.

"That is an uncut diamond," the friend replied in astonishment.

It turned out to be the largest diamond in history. That farm turned out to be one of the richest diamond mines in South Africa.

This short, impactful story is chock full of incredible life lessons. The farmer who sold the property did not know what a diamond looked like in its rough form, so even though he searched for diamonds, he wouldn't know how to recognize one even if he saw one. Diamonds don't appear the way that we see them in the jewelry story. They need to be worked, hammered and polished before they become something of value.

More importantly, the story shows that our treasure is often already right in front of us, but we are too busy looking somewhere else for it. Be it our spouse, our career, or anything else where we find dissatisfaction, the grass is not always greener on the other side. And often when it looks that way, it's because it's fake.

Our best opportunities are often right in front of us. We just need a new way to look at them, or find a new application to polish them into something of value.

Are you able to see any "Acres of Diamonds" in your life? Is there something that looks like a regular rock that can be polished into a gem? Something that is unique to you that you overlook, downplay, or don't make valuable?

Build a Network

"The rich look to build their network. Everyone else looks for a job."— **Robert Kiyosaki**

Starting a new business is challenging. It can consume your thoughts and play on your fears. Most people quit before they start. And when they do push forward, their first question is almost always the same.

"Where do I start?"

One of the best lessons Elizabeth and I learned about starting a business happened by accident. We had an eighteen-month window before we would be moving to Pittsburgh, so there wasn't an immediate time worry, but we wanted to get the ball rolling. We cold contacted photographers in the Pittsburgh region we thought we could have a connection with. We were hesitant at first because the photography community in Evansville kept mainly to themselves, and we feared Pittsburgh might be the same. We often tried to build a local referral network, but we encountered a greater sense of competition than collaboration.

But with a new reality facing us, we scoured the websites of more than one hundred photographers in and around Pittsburgh. After sending out introduction emails to fifty of them, we got responses back from around fifteen photographers. The other call to action we made was to invest the majority of our time on SEO and getting our website visible in Pittsburgh. It took a few months, but we were ascending high enough in the rankings to finally get some inquiries.

Through those months, we formed a connection with a handful of those photographers we reached out to.

During our trips to Pittsburgh looking at houses, we often met those photographers for coffee or lunch while in town. A group of friendships were formed while looking for a business contact. At the same time, inquiries for weddings in Pittsburgh trickled into our inbox. Being that we hadn't moved yet and the travel would be too difficult for our young family, we turned them down. But the timing was perfect because we had a few new friends in Pittsburgh to send them to.

This continued for a few months, and those clients often booked our new friends for their wedding. They were grateful for the work and promised to return the favor if they could. As our time to move approached, something noticeable changed. We began receiving more inquiries referred from these photographers in Pittsburgh than from online searches. We had given to them, and they gave back. On the morning after we moved, I met with and booked a high-end wedding sent to us by one of the members of our new network. The power of patience, connection, and long-term planning combined to teach us a lesson we never would have learned had we not reached out.

When new photographers reach out to us about starting or growing their business, it's common for them to ask for help. They either want to work for us, have us teach them, or follow along on a shoot. What few do is to reach out and try to add value. If eighteen months earlier I would have emailed those photographers and asked for something, the message would have been ignored or met with a critical eye.

By giving first, we never had to ask. We reached out to them, and then gave them business. If I had planned it out that way, I would have mistakenly thought I had a brilliant business mind, but it was a wonderful fluke. The network is still in full force today and growing stronger. It was built by reaching out and giving without expectation. Not surprisingly, our business grew bigger and faster the second time than it did the first. Unfortunately, we were a contributing reason why the first network didn't build in Indiana. As I reflect back, I didn't approach that first situation with generosity. I wanted connections with people who could help us, even though I would not have admitted that then. My lack of transparency had to be obvious simply because of my mind-set. I looked to get, and then give; not give, and then maybe get.

Give first, without expectation, was the valuable lesson learned. Most importantly, two of those photographers we blindly reached out to are now two of my closest friends. So, the benefits of building a network go far beyond money. They go toward what truly matters in life: relationships.

Nobody Starts Off Great at Anything

If you are in the exciting, scary position of starting out in this crazy freelance world, remember this: nobody starts off great at anything.

In the 1980's, the MTV Video Music Awards was a big deal to teenagers like myself. I stared intently at the screen watching the performances by the musicians, but also to see who would take home coveted awards like 'Video of the Year' and the 'Viewer's Choice Award'. In 1987, in between performances by Madonna, Prince, and Bon Jovi, the presentation for 'Best New Artist in a Video' was set to be announced. All the bands up for the award, including Bruce Hornsby and The Georgia Satellites, were fresh faces that had just recently been thrust into the mainstream music scene.

After the band Crowded House was named the winner, lead singer Neil Finn gave an interview to MTV. With a bubbly laugh, the interviewee asked Finn how it felt to be the 'Best New Artist'. Finn's smile turned sarcastically serious and he gave a brief answer that confused me.

"Well, we get to pretend like we're new for a year."

As the interview concluded, I remember being unsure why he said that. What did he mean? Being that I was never a fan of the band, I unconsciously filed that moment in the back of my mind and didn't remember it for years. But during many instances of change during my life, I would think back on what Finn briefly mentioned that night. As I plugged away at my career, connections naturally grew. There was always someone new checking us out, hiring us, or forming a relationship with us—and I'd hear the same sort of comment over and over.

"This is Vincent. He's the new…"

And I would feel the same way Finn must have felt that night. I'm not new, I would think to myself. I've been doing this for years. But to them, I was new. And to the MTV audience, so was Crowded House. But his story didn't start when they filmed Don't Dream It's Over, the video that won the award that night. Finn and Crowded House drummer Paul Hester started playing in a band together called Split Enz, in 1975.

After eight years, the band split up (pun intended) and Finn was approached to join a band called The Mullanes. The Mullanes then morphed into Crowded House. Because of Split Enz's popularity in Australia during those eight years, Crowded House already had an established fan base.

Even with their larger-than-usual following, their record company barely gave Crowded House any promotion. Their first single on the new album went nowhere. But when their second single, Don't Dream It's Over, was released in late 1986— more than eleven years after Split Enz started—it become an international hit.

The song went to number two in the United States and number one in Canada. Three months later, they were onstage at the ARIA music awards for 'Best New Talent', 'Song of the Year', and 'Best Video'. Not long after that came the MTV Video Music Awards. Split Enz weren't voted best new artist in 1975. It took eleven years for Neil Finn and Crowded House to win that title for 'Best New Artist'.

Nobody starts off great at anything, but starting is vital if you ever want to become great.

Expect the Unexpected

In 1998, I received a phone call from Tom Buchanan, the lead photographer for the World Wrestling Federation. My co-worker, John Giamundo, recommended me to Tom for a freelance gig. Tom needed a photographer experienced with sports to shoot and light arenas for major events, which I had been doing with the National Hockey League.

Tom threw me right into the fire, hiring me for a three-day WWF tour to Milwaukee, Rockford, Illinois, and finally Chicago, with fellow shooters Rich Freeda and David McLain. It was a bizarre scene to be part of this traveling circus, but I was astonished by how professional the operation was backstage. When you put that many personalities with egos and money together in a traveling show, there is bound to be drama, but to me, as a newcomer, the operation seemed seamless.

In Milwaukee, which was a live pay-per-view show, I was essentially a grunt. Running around getting whatever Rich, David, or Tom needed. Either hustling up to the catwalks to set up a transmitter or adjusting the soft boxes for Rich to do a portrait of World Champion "Stone Cold" Steve Austin. That was my gig. The next night, in Rockford, I would be shooting live at ringside.

In situations like this, where three or four photographers are working and traveling consistently with each other, camaraderie is key. Tom was mild-mannered, and we hit it off right away. David—a contract photographer for National Geographic—was thoughtful, genuine, and fun.

Rich, Tom's lead photographer, was louder and more gruff. More like me. We didn't argue at first, but there was more tension between us. Tom told me to stand up to him and not take his crap, which I appreciated.

In Rockford, we set up for a photo shoot with Dustin Runnels (aka Goldust), in the backstage studio. Runnels is the son of wrestling legend Dusty Rhodes, one of the most successful professional wrestlers from the previous generation. With his face painted gold, standing 6'6" and weighing 243 pounds, he was an intimidating presence with a demeanor to match. Very surly and abrupt, I was warned to stay away from him.

Rich finished the shoot with a Polaroid back to test the lighting. As Runnels finished his prematch meal at catering, Rich sent me over with the Polaroid to see what Dustin thought about the look of the image. I walked over and handed it to him, which should have been a formality. He looked at the Polaroid, and then looked back at me.

"This looks like crap," he yelled, only with more colorful language. He crumpled the image in his giant hands and threw it at me. Dumbfounded, I picked it up off the floor and walked back to the makeshift studio. I told Tom and Rich what happened, and they reassured me that it was just Dustin being Dustin.

The beginning of a WWF show is intense. Pyrotechnics explode throughout the arena as the crowd gets whipped into a frenzy. The photographers check transmitters and test lights. We wore headsets to communicate with the TV cameramen and producers, so we know who is about to enter and where to stay away from (so we don't get blown to pieces by a pyro blast). Preparing to walk toward the ring, Tom and I talked through last-minute details. That's when I felt a giant slap on my back. I turned around to find Goldust staring down at me.

"Do you work here full-time?" he boomed.

"I'm on contract," I stammered. "Ummm… not full-time."

"If I ever see you here again," he said, glaring into my eyes, "I'm going to kill you."

There was no joking. No smirk. I looked at Tom, who uncomfortably motioned me to move toward ringside as the show started. I did not want to go, and he could see it on my face.

"Don't think about it," he shouted in my ear while lifting my headset, the pyro for the show opening exploding above our heads. The show began, but all I could think about was this giant dude who wanted to rip my head off. To make matters worse, he was scheduled for the fourth match of the card, meaning we would be right next to each other in less than an hour. I tried not to think about it, but failed miserably.

The moment I was not waiting for arrived all too soon.

"Enter Goldust," a producer's voice crackled through my headset, and I immediately looked toward Tom shooting from the other side of the ring. I was hoping he would tell me to bolt for one match. I mean, really, it was just one match. And this guy wanted to kill me. Tom put his hands up, motioning for me to stay put. It was not the answer I was looking for, but I did feel safe. We were on national television. What could he really do to me while the cameras were rolling?

Goldust strolled toward the ring, brushing past me. After the bell sounded, Goldust put his opponent in a headlock and looked my way. With a sinister smile, he looked into my eyes again. At that moment, I realized that being on live TV wasn't a good thing. I've seen wrestlers use photographers as props before. They grab their camera and take photographs, or even get them involved in the match. All in the fun of the show, of course. He could pull me into the ring if he liked. Who would stop him? And if I was in there, he had the option of hurting me. If I was in pain, how would anyone know? Everyone looks like they are in pain at that point. It's part of selling the show.

The match couldn't have been more than ten minutes. It felt like ten days. With every move, I hoped for a pin. I can still remember the sweat pouring off my head during that match. Goldust won the match, left the ring, and didn't pay any attention to me on the way out. He must have forgotten, I thought. To say I took a deep breath would be a severe understatement. The night ended with me still alive. Exhausted from the three-day circus, I flew back home to New York.

The following Sunday, we were to fly to San Antonio and Austin for the next two events. I called Tom to express my concern over what happened, and he said that he hadn't seen anything like that before and would talk to upper management. I didn't see Goldust at the San Antonio show. Tom mentioned that he might be getting punished for what he did to me.

The next day in Austin, I was ringside early in the day setting up as the wrestlers stretched and practiced. David and I were about to go backstage for our meal when Runnels entered the ring, in street clothes.

"You cost me ten grand, brother," Runnels yelled at me for everyone to hear.

"What did I do?" I asked, displaying more courage than I actually felt.

"(Vince) McMahon fined me ten thousand bucks for screwing with you," he answered. "This ain't the end of it, you know!"

And it wasn't. Over the next eighteen months, I worked on contract for the WWF, and he never missed an opportunity to make me uncomfortable. After a while, I was pretty sure he wouldn't hurt me, but I wouldn't have put money on that. Through that time, I went back to school at Ohio University and told Tom that my time with the WWF would be ending. He understood, and he went out of his way to get me work when he could.

A year later, Tom called with a phenomenal assignment. He flew me in for a three-day stint in Albany, New York City, and New Jersey to do a behind-the-scenes documentary about the WWF with nearly unlimited access.

Rich, Dave, and Tom were all there, along with the photographer who replaced me. By the time we got to the Meadowlands in New Jersey, we were all telling stories of the past few years. I had just gotten hired in Evansville, and it was obvious this would be my last gig with this crew. Rich told old stories and went on to describe the ultimate prank they pulled. He had told Goldust about this new photographer, and then got him to say this or do that, to scare him. Laughter boomed out of the room, from me, as well.

Rich told this story as if it ended in Texas. The only problem, I told him, was that they failed to let me know it was a gag. Rich thought they told me, and never knew I lived in fear all that time. A prank that was meant to last a week ended up lasting more than two years. That just made them laugh harder.

I had to learn this lesson the hard way. To expect the unexpected. And to not forget to laugh at myself along the way.

The Easy Button

"Forget about shortcuts. Instead, enjoy the wonders of your path."
—Paulo Coelho

Around seven years ago, I photographed an event with a local DJ. His wife was taking photographs for him.

As the evening progressed, she peppered me with questions about our business, how much money we make per assignment, and how quickly we built it up. It was obvious she was looking for a quick fix. She admitted that she didn't know how to properly use her camera yet. I asked her about her level of photography experience.

She pushed that question aside, and pressed again on the "shortcuts" to getting successful. After I told her that I do business coaching and consulting, she told me she wanted to start a photography business because, as she stated, "That's where the money is."

I told her that I'm not smart enough to figure out the shortcuts, but if you really want to have a great photography business, it helps if you're a great photographer. She then asked what my coaching rates were. After I told her, she asked me a question only someone looking for a quick fix would ask: "How many lessons before I'm a great photographer?"

"I've been at this for sixteen years," I responded. "I'll let you know when I get there."

To no surprise, I never received an email response back. I saw her two years later at an event, but this time she didn't have a camera. I asked how her photography career was going, and she told me that she gave it up a long time ago.

"There's just no money in it," she explained.

If you are looking for an easy button, go to Staples. If you are looking to succeed, don't look for shortcuts.

Talent

"I have no special talent. I am only passionately curious."—**Albert Einstein**

There are few words which annoy me as much as the word 'talent'. Maybe I'm jaded. Scarred a bit, perhaps.

I've been doing this photography thing for the better part of twenty-three years now. More than half my life. A day doesn't go by where someone, somehow, someway tells me that I have talent. It's meant as a compliment, but I know it's not true.

Sounds like a humble thing to say, right? Baloney. Do you want to know how I know I don't have talent? Because here is the definition of talent as described by Webster's Dictionary:

A special ability that allows someone to do something well.

So, when I hear I have talent, I immediately think back to my first few years in photography. From the moment I put a camera strap around my neck until at least two years later, maybe three, not one single human on earth told me I had talent. Not one.

Drive? Yes.

Passion? Sure.

Grit? Uh-huh.

Motivation? Absolutely.

Talent? Meh.

So, if talent is a special ability that allows someone to do something well, shouldn't that have been there from the start? Shouldn't there have been at least a teeny, tiny sign there was an ounce of talent in my body? In my first five years of photography, I made less than twenty thousand dollars combined directly from my craft.

Does that sound like someone with talent? Wouldn't someone—anyone— have seen the gemstone I was and paid me handsomely for it?

Talent is an easy word to throw around because there are an exceptional, rare few who can sit down at a piano and ace it right away, or more commonly, the athlete who possesses that natural skill that is unteachable. But for everyone else, talent is disguised as drive, passion, grit, determination, and motivation.

It turns out that the harder I worked, the more talented people said I was.

The Fear Factor

"Most people don't do what they want because they are afraid."
—Steven Pressfield

I learned something interesting from my friend, Rob. Rob and I have been friends for more than twenty years, and after years of not being in touch often, we began talking weekly about life, business, and family for the past four years.

Having cut his teeth in the news business, he always kept an eye on the news. Many of our conversations focused on the current state of the economy and what things will be like in the future.

Interestingly, when the conversation went in that direction, it seemed to turn negative. Having grown up in the news business, as well, I had developed the ability to block it out. I did my best to focus on positive actions to take, putting inspiring thoughts into my head. It wasn't always easy, particularly in a world of 24/7 connectedness, but I did my best.

Recently, we had a deep conversation about fear. Even though I had been able to stay focused on the task at hand, I also went through an extended period of worry, fear, and anxiety about the unknown. Like Rob, I got caught in an online web of negative news. The more I saw, the more I looked for it. The more I looked, the more frightened I became. The more frightened I became, the more powerless I felt. I became mentally paralyzed. When the future looked hopeless, I could not think of concentrating on the present.

When Rob and I spoke that afternoon, we recounted his recent history. After he was laid off from a well-paid position back in 2009, he went freelance. That wasn't a dream of his; it was simply his only option. He desperately wanted another staff position, but those positions had dried up. The first few years for him were a struggle. With two little girls, he was fortunate that his wife had a full-time job to keep them propped up. Over time, and overcoming his fears, Rob worked on his business. One referral led to another, and three years later, his business was growing steadily.

By the time we had the "fear" talk, he had been freelancing for more than five years. He cautiously relayed to me that the previous year was the best year ever for his business. And the year before was better than the previous one. It had been a steady growth from the start, with the obvious potholes that show up in any endeavor.

But when the conversation turned back to the future, he again was skeptical. Having just gone through this mental hell myself, I pressed him on it for the first time. I needed to get some answers not only for him, but for me.

"It's hard to watch the news and feel positive," he noted, "but I need to stay informed."

The question popped into my head immediately, and I knew that it would reveal an important answer. I just didn't know what it would be.

"If you hadn't watched the news over the past six years, and seeing how your business has done and your life has evolved since then," I asked, "would your view on the economy be positive or negative?"

He gave me an uncomfortable laugh. And then another.

"I'd have to say that everything has gotten better," he answered.

If it wasn't for the news being fed into his head, he would view everything more positively than he currently does, which brought up another interesting point. Through the fear and struggle, Rob was able to improve and grow. But many times it held him back from trying.

After our conversation ended, I wondered—if he could be successful pushing through his fear, how much further along would he be if he hadn't been influenced by any of it? His potential— like all of us—is unlimited. What if he hadn't pushed through it at all? He most likely would have taken a job he did not want simply for the income, and he would be just another in the endless line telling everyone else that their dream is impossible. Now his business is thriving.

The news is not there to make you feel good. The whole point of the news business is to make you feel bad about your life so you buy the things their advertisers are selling. Being a former news guy, this has been a difficult lesson for me. If you felt great after watching the news, you would most likely feel content and happy, which isn't good for business. You wouldn't need to buy their stuff to make you feel better or look better if you were content. Why is it that nearly every advertisement, aside from maybe life insurance, takes place in a bigger, brighter house than yours? Or with a better car? Or a better phone or television? These people aren't dumb. They know that when you watch dreary news and then see an escape, you want to go to that escape.

Learn from Rob. Overcome your fear and fight through it. You determine whether your business, your economy, your life, will be a success. Nothing is possible until your desire for that thing is greater than your fear of it.

Why Do New Small Businesses Fail?

This is the best time in history to start a business, and it's only going to get better. The internet, as you may have heard somewhere, has changed everything.

Most of the small businesses created in the past decade would not have been possible fifteen years ago. Think about that for a second. Our photography business is no different. Only fifteen years ago, we would have had to rely on the Yellow Pages for customers to find us!

Everything has changed so quickly, and it's all lined up perfectly for the freelancer. I can write this book with my four-year-old cuddled next to me. I can run my mastermind group in an hour with like-minded people from all over the world without leaving my home office. I can send out a contract to our newest client in minutes without printing a piece of paper. I can coach through Skype and Zoom. I can receive payments with a few clicks of the mouse, all within minutes.

But if it's such a great time to start a business, why do so many fail? I am often asked: what is the number one thing that kills a new small business?

Lack of good ideas?

Not having enough talent?

Lack of smarts?

Not enough capital to survive the early days?

Lack of connections?

Not enough time?

The answer is… none of the above.

The number one thing that kills a beginning business is not setting aside tax money. Can you believe that? Just like the feds didn't get Al Capone for all the dastardly deeds involved in his crime-ridden enterprise, they got him on tax evasion.

It turns out that not setting aside tax money is the cause for most of the new small business failures.

It's yet another reason to understand and have control of your money.

Where Will I Find Time?

More than money, a lack of time may be your biggest obstacle.

When we started our first business, I would stay up late doing research on how other successful business owners made the transition out of a full-time job. It was during one of these late-night internet sessions that I first read about Parkinson's Law. It is the observation that work expands to fill the time available for its completion. In my bleary, late-night state, I needed to read that a few times to understand it. Essentially, the law states that if you give me three hours to complete a job, I'll find a way to make it last three hours. Never mind the fact that it might be possible to complete in thirty minutes. Guilty as charged, I told myself. I have the ability to waste time like the best of them.

As I dug deeper, I looked into some of the more common time-wasters. That was when I came upon an article by Darren Hardy, author of *The Compound Effect*, about how you can gain more than five hours to your life every day. I shouldn't have even clicked the overdramatic headline because it was obviously an extreme exaggeration. But I was well-trained in this Parkinson's Law idea and was baited into wasting a little more time. I was curious as to what kind of silliness it had in store for me. Should I sleep only three hours a night? Eat one big meal per day and work through the other two to save an hour? Take up speed reading? But the answer was uncomfortbly surprising and obvious.

Turn off my television.

Numerous reports showed that the average American watches more than five hours of television per day. Per day! That hit me, and it hit me hard. As I stared at my computer screen, the television was on in the background. It had been on for a few hours. I spun my chair to get a view of the screen showing the latest political drama unfolding—at 2:00 a.m. on a Tuesday morning. There is always a political drama unfolding to watch. Or a sitcom. Or another movie. Or sports.

Oh, jeez. Sports. How many fall afternoons have I started with the pregame shows and ended asleep in front of the Sunday night game? Subtracting bathroom breaks and getting up for the occasional slice of pizza, I calculated that those days were more than ten hours of tube time.

Five hours a day? The math was just too juicy to pass up. Five hours a day is just a tad more than two thousand hours per year. It also breaks down to 300 minutes each day. What could you accomplish every day with a 300-minute head start on the rest of the world?

Could You Use More Time?

What could you do if, starting tonight, you found an extra five hours in your day? If you spend anywhere close to the amount of time watching television or mindlessly surfing the 'net, you just found the time. If you don't think it's possible, Jeffrey Strain's story might convince you otherwise.

Strain was doing better than the average American. He was only watching three hours of television a day. He made the decision to dramatically cut down on the amount of television he watched and plow that time into creating a website with his friend.

While working his day job, he continued building multiple websites in the extra time he carved out. In three years, Strain and his friend created a string of websites and blogs that allowed them both to quit their jobs and fulfill their dream of self-employment.

"It's amazing the amount you can accomplish when you find an extra 3,285 hours a year to work on something you enjoy doing rather than vegging in front of the TV," Strain said.

Strain is convinced that cutting down on his television time is the difference between him staying in a job he didn't enjoy and having his dream job working for himself.

Television might not just be the costs of the flat-screen on your wall and the monthly cable bill.

It might be costing you the life you desire.

Define Success for Yourself

If you are just getting started, you have a distinct advantage. You have the ability to answer the question that most people never ask themselves before starting their career.

How do you define success?

Is success making gobs of money, but never seeing your children? Is success building a successful online venture, but staring at your phone 24/7 while your kids tug at your pants for your attention? Is success slaving away at a job that feeds your family and keeps a roof over their heads, but provides little else, including your time with them? Is success growing a business so big that it takes you with it? Is success doing what you love, regardless of how it affects those most important to you in life? If having more means it compromises your life with your family and causes them to suffer, that isn't success, it's materialism.

You now have the ability to choose what success is and shape your work to fit your ideal life.

Does Money Buy Happiness?

"Show me someone who thinks money buys happiness, and I'll show you someone who has never had money."—**David Geffen**

One of the saddest things I see are men who are wealthy but have distant or damaged relationships with their children. Quite often, they invested in the wrong thing.

I was talking with an incredibly wealthy gentleman at an event I photographed years back. The fundraiser was held at his gorgeous, sprawling estate with views that would be the envy of any working man or woman. In the few moments I had a chance to talk with him, I complimented him on his home and success. I asked him if he had a piece of business advice he would share with me as we looked to grow ours. He asked me if I had kids. His question seemed odd considering my question, but I responded that I had two little boys with a third on the way.

"If you're looking to do what I've done, I would tell you to pause. Ask yourself why you want more before you begin chasing it." he stated.

Having more isn't a bad thing," he continued. "but if you chase for more and don't know why you're chasing it, you'll be lost. You're soon to have your third little boy? I wouldn't be striving for this," he said, pointing out his vast estate. "I have bank accounts filled with money and a family I don't even know. And I'm eating the same chicken sandwiches you are."

"Do you know what I would tell my younger self, the one with a wife, two little girls, and an insatiable appetite for business and money?" this man said in more of a whisper. "You already have it all. Right now. Keep working hard, keep growing, but don't ever let that become more important than your family. I let it become more important than my family. Now I have a big, gorgeous, beautiful home filled with emptiness and expensive furniture."

That five-minute conversation was more valuable than anything I ever learned in school. It quite possibly was more valuable than everything I ever learned in school.

Make A Life, Not A Living

"Don't let making a living prevent you from making a life."—John Wooden

I recently did a conference call with a multi-millionaire many times over. His income is the envy of everyone around him, but his stress is no different than those same people. Doesn't that seem odd? He gets up at the same time as the commuters rushing for the morning train. He stretches his time to get to the gym for a workout. He makes sure he gets home for dinner most nights to spend some time with his family. There is no doubt his vacations, his home, and his cars are more lavish than most.

But why isn't he in control of his life?

His drive comes from growing his business bigger, which keeps him commuting to the office every day. He feels responsible for the people who work for him, and reducing his involvement would put their jobs at risk. He also doesn't have any other interests besides his business.

He'd love a lifestyle that was more flexible, one where he could spend more time with his family and do the things he loves. As crazy as it sounds, he is stuck. This man has a high income and net worth, but he doesn't enjoy it the way he envisioned he would. The stress is starting to take its toll, as he struggles with his weight and his close relationships.

I constantly hear from those in the low six-figure income range that have a different, but similar, problem.

One family exemplifies the many I consulted. As their income increased, so did their lifestyle. Things that started as a luxury now feel like a necessity. The clothes, the house, the lessons for the kids, the vacations. They're no longer as exciting as they are expected. The thought of cutting them out seems like a giant sacrifice, and their only option appears to be 'make more money'.

On top of it, she would like to quit her job to be home with their kids, but they could no longer afford their house if she cut out her income. So, to keep up, he puts in more overtime, which means less time with his family. She struggles as she watches her friends at home with their kids while she drives her kids to daycare. Each one of these examples told me that they feel overwhelmed by time. They feel as trapped as any debt-strapped employee.

Money will never equal freedom if your lifestyle exceeds your income. It doesn't matter if you are a multi-millionaire, earn $150,000 annually, or make $32,000 a year.

Does your money serve you or master you? Remember, when you gain control of your money, you gain control of your life. Not paying for it now means paying more for the same thing later. If you think it's going to hurt now, it will hurt much more later.

How Can You Impact the World?

I was listening to an interview with the Reverend Billy Graham. I had heard about the famous preacher, but never heard him speak. The Reverend was in his nineties at this point, and he was asked if there was a way he could have had a greater impact on the world.

"I've spoken to 80,000 people inside of stadiums all over the globe," Graham said, "but I've learned that if I had spent more time speaking to my three children instead of stadiums filled with people, I would have had a greater impact on the world."

Talk about putting what matters into perspective. All my big goals were prioritized and compartmentalized after hearing that one line. How many people do you know who gave up what really, truly mattered in their life to pursue something else they thought was more important?

I forced myself to think on that line, and I realized that my main job is being a husband and a dad. That is what I thought about. That is what I would regret later if I didn't do it right. I want to spend as much time loving, supporting and making memories with them as soon as I possibly can.

I worked my butt off before we had kids. We worked like mad to get our business going when they were little. I'm sure I'll devote tremendous amounts of time to work when the kids are grown and on their own. I have no plans to ever retire. I'm passionate about the work I get to do now, but I will not miss these years with our kids.

There is such a tremendous satisfaction in working, creating, contributing, and helping others, but this time—the time when our kids are living in our house—is sacred. No matter what advertisements or your over-extended friends tell you, kids do not care about money. Kids care about time. They want you to spend time with them.

The money lesson we learned from this was astounding. By valuing so preciously our family time, we had no choice but to put a high value on our work time. It was then that we finally had the guts to charge what we felt we were worth. And the market didn't blink an eye. Our rates went higher, reflecting our experience, hustle, talent, and availability, and the market rewarded us for it.

Rates went higher and the bookings came quicker. It made no sense in my mind. What we didn't understand was that when we valued our time, others did, too.

We counted on having more time with the family and were fine with the consequence of having less money. There would always be time to make more money, but how long did we have to build Legos with the most adorable eight-year-old in the universe? It turned out that we got the time we desired with the kids and wound up making significantly more money than before, even while working dramatically less hours. That leverage compounded into the freedom to be choosy about what work we took, with the added ability to turn down lucrative assignments if they didn't fit into our plan.

If you don't value your time, do not expect those hiring you to value it either.

20 Questions

To conclude each of the stages, we will finish off with 20 questions to gauge where you are at during each stage in your journey toward freedom.

1. Are you a part of the 80% of Americans who dislike their jobs?
2. What parts of your life do you believe you are 100% correct, but you could be wrong?
3. Figure out your FRUIT. Add up the cost of your food, residence, utilities, insurance, and transportation, plus a little for entertainment. What is that number?
4. How much debt do you have, not including a mortgage?
5. Do you have a mortgage? If so, what is the balance?
6. How much is in your emergency fund?
7. Have you had an idea for a business that won't go away?
8. Do you have a network of friends, colleagues, and associates to build off of?
9. What can you do daily to grow and nurture that network?
10. Where is your Acre of Diamonds?
11. What area in life do people tell you that you have talent in?
12. What fear is holding you back from getting started on your business? If you already have a business, what is holding you back from growth?
13. Can you envision using all of your business profits to pay down your debts?
14. To gain a five-hour head start per day, are you willing to turn off the television and get off the internet unless it's scheduled and productive?
15. As you look forward, define what success looks like to you in business.
16. Do you believe that money buys happiness?
17. What does success look like with your family?
18. What does success look like with your health?
19. If you've already started a side business, are you bringing in 10% of your FRUIT yet?
20. How can you impact the world?

PHASE II

THE SIDE HUSTLE

I t is projected that in less than ten years, 50% of the population will be self-employed. Not learning the ropes of self-employment now leads to being on the wrong side of the massive divide of income. This country—this world, in fact—is moving toward a workforce of freelancers.

Depending on how you look at it, that can be a scary thought. If you went through twelve years of school, four years of college, and another two years for an advanced degree, the idea of working for yourself might be frightening. Traditional schooling is designed to make us think like an employee, not an entrepreneur or freelancer.

But what is a freelancer, anyway? It's been made out to be a bad word, but as Justin Timberlake might say, I want to bring sexy back to the freelance world.

When we talk of self-employment, the word used most often is entrepreneur. That seems to be the big goal. The cold, hard fact is that most self-employed people are freelancers, not entrepreneurs. Although I will get deeper into that in a bit, know that there is a big difference between the freelancer and the entrepreneur.

For the true entrepreneurs out there, freelancing is unappealing. A successful entrepreneur starts businesses to sell them. A freelancer is self-employed, but does much of the work themselves. Freelancers tend to be of the 'Lone Wolf' mentality, wanting isolation and control over their work. They aren't as interested in growing their business to scale so they can sell to someone else.

They want to do what they love without a boss telling them what to do every day. They don't want to go into an office or factory every day doing the same thing. They want to have more control over their schedule. Time and love of work are just as important as money to the freelancer.

Mark Cuban's Advice for the Self-Employed

"If you're starting a business and you're taking out a loan," Mark Cuban told Bloomberg TV host Trish Regan, "you're a moron."

"There are so many uncertainties involved with starting a business, but the one certainty is that you will have to pay back your loan. The bank doesn't care about your business, so it's a complete conflict. Ninety-nine percent of small business you can start with no capital. It's more about effort. Most businesses don't fail from a lack of capital, they fail from a lack of brains and a lack of effort. Most people just aren't willing to put in the time to work smart. They go for it in a lot of cases, but they don't realize how much work is involved. If you start a business, you better know your industry better than anyone in the whole wide world because you are competing. And if you think anyone you are competing with is going to let you come in and take their business, obviously that's naive. Most people don't recognize that."

What does Cuban think about the trials and tribulations of getting started in business?

"The thing about being an entrepreneur is to just go after it. It's all up to you. A lot of people like to make excuses—I don't have connections, I don't have money— but if you find something you like to do or love to do, go be great at it and see if you can turn it into a business. The worst case, you are going to have fun doing what you love, and best case you can turn it into a business. I'm just not big on excuses. Everyone has the opportunity to do it—you just have to go for it."

Pretty opinionated advice, don't you think? All you have to do is google this story and read the comments to see the amount of pushback Cuban gets from his advice not to take out a loan. There are pages and pages of it. It's also scattered with random examples of successful businesses that started with a loan. I'd argue that you can read stories of countless lottery winners, but that doesn't make it a wise decision to play the lottery. Mathematically, you have a greater chance of being struck by lightning twice than winning the lottery.

The common complaint to his theory is, "Where do you find money to start a business if you can't take out a loan?" Fifty percent of businesses start with less than $1,000, and sixty percent start with less than $5,000.

Own It

Humans have one unifying idea: we all want to control our own destiny.

To start on a new path, it's essential to leave the old ones behind. What got you where you are will not get you where you want to go. The excuses we make to justify where we are in life is nothing but loser talk. I don't write any of this out of theory, but example. As my dad profoundly pointed out in my early years, I was the king of justification.

"You should become a lawyer," he would say in a state of exasperation. "You have an excuse for everything."

One Saturday night when I was twelve years old, my parents went out to dinner with friends, and their son Danny and I stayed at our house to watch wrestling on television. We quickly became bored and decided that lighting plastic rulers on fire in the den would be more fun.

Somehow, my parents didn't notice the smell of burnt plastic after returning home, but my dad did notice an uncomfortable pinch when he sat on the couch while reading the Sunday paper the next morning. While I ate breakfast a few feet away, he pulled out a handful of charred pieces of plastic wedged between the couch cushions.

Mom and Dad went into full freak-out mode. I buried my head in Fruity Pebbles. You didn't need to be a private investigator to figure out what happened. They went on and on about how the house could have burned down; how we could have been killed. Pressed for an answer, I became the consummate politician.

"It was Danny," I said calmly. "He wanted to do it. I didn't want to. I tried to get him to stop…"

They cut me off before I could lie any further, but I didn't budge. It was all Danny, according to me. They were on the phone with his parents within minutes, and on the other end Danny told his side of the story. We both thought it would be fun.

"Nope, nope, nope, not me. I wouldn't do that." I was adamant. I knew I was lying. My parents knew I was lying. I knew my parents knew I was lying. I so badly wanted to be right that I wasn't concerned with the consequences.

I never saw Danny again after that night.

But I didn't learn my lesson. I didn't learn how to 'Own It' for more than a decade after that. Everything was always someone or something else's fault. My teacher, my brother, my parents, my girlfriend, the weather, my boss, the customer. Anyone, or anything, but me.

Of course, life changed when I started to own it. My life sucked not because of my boss, but because of me. I had no money because of me, not my hourly rate. People didn't trust me not because they were out to get me, not because of my actions. I was where I was in life because of what I did to get there. Trust me, I tried blaming everyone else.

To start on the right path, stop blaming others. Stop blaming circumstances. Stop blaming the politicians. If you truly want to move onward and upward, start here. Take 100% responsibility for your life, even if it's not entirely your fault. It will free you up to become trusted, reliable, and a better person. It will free you of your need to be right. Would you rather be right, or successful?

Just own it.

The Game of Risk

"Never risk something you need for something you don't need."
—**Warren Buffett**

The insidious thing about risk is most of the time we don't know we are doing it, and it's what keeps so many of us stuck. Most people wouldn't consider taking a job risky, would they? It's noble to work. It's essential to pay the bills. But what if we increase our debt because we got a raise? Even though we don't want to be in that job. Even though we know there is something bigger for us.

Most people do exactly what Buffett suggests not to do. They risk something they need (dreams, time, health, sanity) for something they don't need (nicer cars, fancier clothes, entertainment, unhealthy foods). And they come in such small bites it just seems normal. After all, all our friends are doing it.

So, you remain stuck in a position you don't want be in, only with bigger bills and a bigger lifestyle that now appears like a need, not a want. It's the crazy cycle that leads to a life of 'kind of' nice stuff, big piles of debt, little time, high stress, and a highly mortgaged house along The Boulevard of Broken Dreams.

Get Paid for Results, Not Time

"Working for someone else will keep you poor."
—**Dan Miller**

When you think of millionaires, who comes to mind? I would guess an actor, musician, or professional athlete would be the first person most people think of. Would it surprise you to learn that all the millionaire actors, athletes, musicians, and celebrities comprise less than 1% of all the millionaires in the United States?

Crazy, right? You would never know that by what we see on television and the inter webs. So, who are all these millionaires? According to the book, The

Millionaire Next Door by Thomas Stanley, 75% percent of millionaires in the United States are self-employed. Seventy-five percent!

We will dig into this fascinating figure later, but the big question now is, "Why is it so hard to become financially set working for someone else?"

It's actually pretty simple. They own you.

Your bosses don't want you to see it that way, but when it comes to your time and work, they own you. Your great ideas are owned by the company. You're busting your hump to come up with solutions to problems that will make them wealthy and make you a living. They pay you a salary, or an hourly wage. while your mind, ideas, and time belong to the company. I'm not suggesting that there is any ill intent of evilness on their part, although, unfortunately, sometimes there is. It's just that you traded that for your time, ideas, and vision for a salary and security.

It also goes deeper than that. It's not just about the work you did at the office anymore. If you signed an intellectual property agreement, they can claim they own anything you wrote, created, or thought of while you worked there. Employers have claimed the rights to employees' Facebook, Twitter, LinkedIn, and other social media content. This goes all the way down to your social media following. If you have built a large audience while under their employment, many companies now demand lower severance pay in exchange for you keeping your following.

Rich Dads and Poor Dads

I had never picked up a money or business book before starting our business. Instead of spending my lunch hour messing around, I started scanning through the business section at Barnes & Noble. One of those comfortable, oversized chairs on the second level became my spot. *Rich Dad, Poor Dad* by Robert Kiyosaki grabbed my attention. I was a poor dad who wouldn't mind eventually being a rich dad.

The book, I learned later, is highly controversial. It is the story of a young man whose father struggled financially. His best friend's father was one of the wealthiest businessmen on their island in Hawaii. The friend's father taught the boy all about how money works while his own father struggled in a government job.

Critics question the validity of whether some of the people in the book even existed, or if the author had any of the assets he wrote about prior to the book being published. Regardless, one of the chapters was a cornerstone in helping me believe that we could—and should—be self-employed. The chapter discusses the difference between assets and liabilities, and thinking back to high-school economics, I came close to falling asleep. But then the book went into the way the tax codes are structured, and how owning a corporation has such a tremendous tax advantage over being an employee. As a struggling employee looking to start a corporation, I woke up.

He gave a simple description that was crystal clear: employees earn money, then are taxed on it, and then get the rest. Corporations earn money, spend it on anything related to the business, and then get taxed on the rest. I looked at our job and our new business in a completely different light. I saw an immediate $20,000 advantage we would have gained by being self-employed instead of being employees.

No wonder it was so difficult to forge ahead financially as an employee. Whether I agree or disagree politically, these were the laws in place, and they highly influenced us becoming self-employed.

The Investment

Freelance to Freedom is not an investment book. There are so many books that go into great detail on the best options for stocks, investing, and everything Wall Street related. I do, however, want to touch briefly on the options afforded to you as a freelancer.

Why is this an important topic for you? In 2015, a survey done by the Freelance Union and Elance-oDesk, discovered that thirty-four percent of the nation's workforce is now freelancing— roughly fifty-three million Americans. And that number is only going higher.

Sadly, nearly forty million working-age households have no retirement savings at all, and of those who do, they do not have nearly enough saved, according to the National Institute on Retirement Security.

This is a dangerous alley to be walking down. And you are walking through this dark alley alone. As a freelancer, you actually need to do better than the average employee at investing because you don't have the comfort of a company-backed 401(k) match or pension. Heck, even employees don't have most of that comfort anymore.

Are you like most freelancers who think saving and investing for retirement is too complicated? But what if the truth was that even starting small is much simpler than you think, and it will give you greater peace of mind and help you spend less on taxes every year?

There are a few options which are ideal for the self-employed. I am going to break this down into my favorite options, all of which we personally use.

Solo 401(k)

The Solo 401(k) is specifically designed for small business entities with only one owner, or husband-spouse partnership. The Solo 401(k) has a high contribution limit, up to $59,000 annually. If a spouse is a planned participant, they can also make contributions. You also have the option to make a contribution of up to 25% of your business earnings. As with all these options, you have the freedom to contribute as little or as much as you want.

SEP-IRA

The SEP (Simplified Employee Pension) is very easy to set up. They are available at almost all banks, requires only a one-page form, and you can open it and fund it right up until your tax-filing deadline. All the money contributed to your SEP will grow tax deferred. That means you get a tax deduction the year you file, but you will pay taxes when you take the money out. Contribution limits in 2016 are $53,000 annually.

ROTH IRA

Roth IRA's make tons of sense if you expect your tax rate to be higher in retirement than it is currently. Which means the younger you are, the more they make sense. The contribution limits are $5,500 a year for 2016, but they are not tax deferred, so you get no tax savings that year. But the best part is that they grow tax free, so when you do take the money out, it's all yours!

This is just a small guide, and you will need to do the research for what works best for you. But the key, like everything else, is to just get started.

And don't believe the media and cultural hype that the little man can't get ahead. These plans are set up and designed for anyone who is self-employed to increase wealth, pay less taxes, and become one of those awful rich people we all love to bash.

Are You an Entrepreneur or Freelancer?

"I want to start my own business like you," I hear often. "I want to be an entrepreneur."

Not a week goes by where someone doesn't say a variation of that line to me. Elizabeth and I are celebrating our twelfth business anniversary, and we realized recently that we weren't entrepreneurs. That was hard to accept. Doesn't running our own business successfully automatically make us entrepreneurs?

Seth Godin, arguably the most brilliant business mind of our time, set me straight during the Business Gets Personal conference in New York City.

Godin explained the difference between being an entrepreneur and a freelancer. The word freelancer sounded so much less impressive. I am a freelancer on newspaper and magazine assignments, but I'm an entrepreneur, I assured myself. Most of us freelancers think we're entrepreneurs. Godin related that freelancers get paid when they work, but when they don't work, they don't get paid.

Hmmmm.

Entrepreneurs, on the other hand, build a business larger than themselves so they get paid when they sleep. Entrepreneurs can sell their business easily because the business isn't related to what they do all day.

Ouch.

As successful as our little craft had become, we couldn't sell it if we tried. It one hundred percent relied on us. Heck, the business name is made up of both our first names, Elizabeth Vincent Photography. Unless we line up a husband-wife photography team with our style and our names, we've built ourselves a job, not a business.

I shifted in my seat. This was getting uncomfortable. It was as if he was talking to me directly. Inside the elegant Rose Theatre at Lincoln Center, Seth Godin taught me that I wasn't an entrepreneur—yet. I'm a freelancer. We get paid when we work. So how in the world have we stayed in business this long without realizing this?

Apparently, we've been exceptional freelancers. The way to make it as a freelancer, he explained, is to be exceptional at it. And the market for exceptional freelancers has never been better. If you are exceptional, people will find you. That has always been our subconscious philosophy. Aside from our first year in the game, we'd never advertised. We'd never done bridal shows or organized networking events. We always relied on word of mouth, which can only happen with happy customers.

Godin noted that the market for average freelancers is awful. There is always someone cheaper if they're looking for average. The race you run becomes a race to the bottom. And that's a race you do not want to win.

Our business path was finally making sense. Elizabeth and I honed our photography craft at various newspapers for a decade before we ventured to take on our own clients. That, in itself, made us different. Who hones a craft for ten years before going into business? That fact should have alerted us that we weren't a natural fit for entrepreneurship. We both loved creating the work. Selling it was a different story.

But it set us up perfectly for being exceptional freelancers, although we were freelancers pretending we were entrepreneurs.

Freelancers who pretend to be entrepreneurs always hire the cheapest freelancer, Godin added.

And that freelancer will always be you. And it most certainly was us. We did the graphic design because we were the cheapest freelancer. We did the post-production work. We did the meetings, the research for products, and the budget. We did the troubleshooting on our website at 3:00 a.m. when we had an 8:00 a.m. assignment the next morning. Entrepreneurs, Godin, explained, build an asset outside themselves. We hadn't done that. There is nothing wrong with being a freelancer, he explained to me later in person. Just don't confuse the two.

So, if you are one of the many who are fired up about starting your own business, know the difference between being a freelancer and an entrepreneur. It can be one of the greatest lessons you learn before you start. Fortunately for us, the ten years honing our craft was what we loved doing. It turned out to be on-the-job preparation for the next stage in our careers.

After hearing Godin speak, I immediately realized the plethora of mistakes we made throughout our time in business. We hired ourselves too many times because we were the cheapest freelancers around. That wiped us out mentally and physically. We should have been doing more of the work we loved and fewer of the tasks that came with it. It took up valuable time where we could have been growing the business, creating ideas and building something that didn't entirely depend on us doing the work.

What Do You Love?

My fifth-grade midterm report card was a list of mediocrity and sadness. If anything confirmed the utter averageness of my early existence, this sterile green piece of carbon paper did the trick. There were eighty columns for my teacher to choose: excellent, satisfactory, or needs improvement. The report card covered a wide swath of math, reading, science, and social studies. That paper gave a thorough evaluation on my place in the class hierarchy and my future possibilities in the free world.

While my eyes scanned down the sheet as my bus pulled away from East Hills Elementary School, it began to sink in that my future was not going to be held in high regard at this institution.

I started at the top left and quickly looked down, searching for my first "excellent" check. Twelve "satisfactories" and six "needs improvements" later, I scrolled slower. When I made it to the bottom of the first column without one excellent mark, the idea of hiding under my seat until the next morning started to creep in. I didn't look at any boxes except for "excellent" in the second column, and time flew. I made it to the bottom without one excellent checkmark. Not even an obligatory one for gym. *If I earned excellence in anything, I thought to myself, it was during that floor hockey game where I scored four goals.* My teacher must have been drinking coffee in the lounge during that athletic display.

It was not possible to be more average. At the bottom was a brief note from my teacher. She wrote that I was a smart boy, which felt like a girl saying you're cute after rejecting you for a date eighty times. My teacher mentioned how I had difficulty concentrating, and the only subject I was interested in was sports. When my parents read it back to me, I couldn't argue. I daydreamed during class by drawing team logos, or writing the names of the New York Mets players, or drawing a map with the names of all the stadiums. When I got home, I created cutout mini versions of different stadiums, coloring in the seats and making the field as green as it looked on television. It was infinitely more interesting to me than school.

The next time I saw that report card was more than thirty years after that depressing afternoon on the yellow bus. I was at my brother's home in New York. After taking a few minutes to reflect, I put the paper down to finish the presentation I was working on about my twenty-year career as a professional sports photographer and the book I was creating about my travels around the country photographing games in every professional stadium in the United States. The timing of that encounter—and the irony of it—seemed way too good to be true.

On the ride to give my presentation, I wondered what would have happened if I believed that report card. What would my life be like today if I accepted that I was just average? How many incredible relationships, experiences, accomplishments, and memories would have never happened if I listened to that little green piece of paper and the teacher who didn't look beyond the rules to see what one of her students actually loved to do?

Decide What You Don't Want to Do

Back in high school, I drove my guidance counselor crazy. Our talks usually concluded with her face contorted into confusion or annoyance. I had the ability to make those looks appear on my parents' faces, as well. It was my senior year, and we were talking inside her dark, cramped office lit only by a small, orange desk lamp. We were discussing college majors that might be appropriate for me.

Judging by my grades, my options were limited, and I had little interest in the few she recommended. She became visibly irritated as I shuffled around inattentively in the stiff chair.

"So," she barked, raising her voice slightly to get my full attention, "what do you want to do with your life?"

"I don't have a clue what I want to do," I replied honestly. "But I know what I don't want. I don't want to wear a tie to some office every day."

Rubbing her head in frustration, she excused me from her office.

As silly as it may sound, that one decision to not want a wear a tie is a giant reason why I am able to write this book today.

So often we only think about what we want to do, or how much money we want to make in a career, or a field which is hiring the most people. But nobody ever asks what we don't want to do. I did not want to wear a tie to an office every day. Even at sixteen years old, I was as sure of that then as I am today. With that one choice, many jobs were off the table for me. I would not become an accountant, a lawyer, Dilbert, or any job related to a cubicle. In college, I bounced around between various majors not involving tying a piece of cloth around my neck before eventually signing up for photography classes. I knew immediately that this was a career I needed to pursue.

It was only because I chose what I didn't want that I was able to finally find what I did want.

Do I Say Yes to Everything?

Starting a side business comes with all sorts of dilemmas and obstacles. One of the most common concerns is the fear of saying no to new work. It is undoubtedly a tough spot to be in. Remember, it's always difficult before it's easy.

As we progress in this book, I will be an advocate for increasing prices, valuing your worth as well as your work, and freeing up time to make your business and your family life ideal. But when you start out, you need to grind it out.

If you still have a full-time position, you have an advantage. If you are able to successfully reduce your lifestyle to free up cash, even better. At this point, you need to say yes early and often. Lower-paying gigs aren't always a death trap.

Just because you start at a lower rate in the freelance world doesn't mean you are doomed to it.

I can't even count the number of budding freelancers who dug in their heels on a rate because it's the industry standard while wringing their hands while not getting the work.

They stuck with the notion that if they start low, they will be pigeon-holed into those prices forever. Nothing could be further from the truth. And nobody is going to hire you just because of the industry standard. They are going to hire you because they know, like, and trust you.

There are times in the beginning where you need to check your ego at the door and go make something happen. Later on, as your portfolio, connections, and experience expand, you will have given yourself the options to increase your rates and be pickier about the people you work with. And you probably will never work with those beginning clients again, though in the early stages, you will work with some doozies. Just remember them, because they could make you famous later on…

John at the Bar Is a Friend of Mine

Piano Man was Billy Joel's first single, and arguably the song he is most known for. The story behind the song is fascinating.

A struggling, up-and-coming artist in the early '70s, Joel took a six-month gig at a Los Angeles lounge as the piano singer. There have been tons of stories written about how the song came about, and Joel said the song was based upon his experiences during that gig. Additionally, he noted that all the characters in the song were real people who were regulars in the bar.

As he played night after night, he took note of his surroundings. He pointed out the beer-infested microphone. He assessed that being alone was worse than being a lonely person drinking with other lonely people. He brought the angst of regret and inaction into the story, telling the brief saga of John, the humorous, helpful bartender who dreams of life as a movie star.

That story is poignant because it stares at the contrast between him and Joel. Although struggling with a low-paying gig, Billy Joel was chasing his dream and was on the cusp of superstardom. Each time I hear that song, I wonder about John at the bar, and if he ever took the chance to become a movie star. Sadly, it's more likely he continued on at the bar, telling each of the new lounge acts about how he knows that he can make it as an actor without ever taking a shot.

This song is one that never gets stale to me, and that's not just because it was part of an impromptu sing-a-long at our wedding. There are so many life lessons baked into it. Out of all the stories or interviews I have heard about the song, one quote really sticks out.

"If I'm going to do this gig, I am leaving here with a song," Joel remembered.

That quote struck me more about life than about the song. He knew the job was crappy. He knew the pay was low and the conditions were awful—but he was going to come out of it with a song.

I couldn't help but wonder if Joel's mindset was just as important as his musical skill. If he had been thinking more about his own situation, would he have remembered those stories of the people around him? Chances are, he wouldn't have. He would be like almost everyone else and only thinking about how cruddy the pay was. Piano Man never would have been written, and Joel's career might have never taken off.

And years later, he might be lamenting to a different lounge bartender that he knows he could sell out Madison Square Garden twelve straight nights and sell more than 150 million records if he could get out of this place.

Who Needs Insurance?

When I received a phone call from the photo desk at the Associated Press asking if I owned a tuxedo, I knew I was in for an interesting night. The photo editor asked if I would be up for a late night photographing the watch party for the last episode of *Seinfeld* at a restaurant in Rockefeller Center in Manhattan. Afterwards, I would be photographing Al Yeganeh, the "Soup Nazi", at his store on West 55th in Manhattan.

It was a night for the ages, being that *Seinfeld* was my favorite television show. Jerry and the main characters were in Los Angeles for the finale, but the secondary characters were there. Wayne Knight, who played Newman; Steve Hytner, who played Kenny Bania; and Barney Martin, who portrayed Jerry's dad, Morty, were part of the group that gathered to take in the last episode together.

I arrived at the AP office, which was only blocks from the party, to gather the information for the assignment and get whistled at by my coworkers who had never seen me in remotely presentable clothes before. "He cleans up nicely" had never been said about me so many times in one day. I left there thinking I needed to update my appearance.

The party didn't happen quite the way they explained it to me. The cast members sat together at a large table while I looked to capture their reactions to the show. It turned out to be a dicey situation because one of the cast members didn't want me there.

I did my best to be discreet, but Wayne Knight kept giving me a dirty look. Being the most recognizable cast member, it was important to get photographs of him. Walking the tightrope, I took a break and tried working around him when I did fire off the occasional frame. I saw Steve and Barney look at each other and laugh at a scene halfway through the show. I shot one frame when Knight jumped out of his chair.

"Can you get out of here so we can watch our show?" he screamed at me so that everyone could hear.

My eyes widened as I slinked down, giving an uncomfortable smile as I slowly backed up. Not sure what to do, I just froze. He turned toward the television. So did I. I was in no position to disagree with him or try to explain myself. If I couldn't do my job there, which I was invited to, I might as well watch the last episode.

After the show ended, I made my way to the Soup Nazi. As much as he complained about the exposure from *Seinfeld*, Yeganeh was part of a shoot that night with QVC selling his soup. He snapped at me once or twice while shooting, fitting into his character on the show.

Walking back to the AP office, I had no idea that the whole *Seinfeld* experience was just the appetizer to the main course of excitement for the evening. After processing and scanning my film, I offered to give my friend and photographer Ed Betz and our nighttime photo editor, Mike Kopec, a ride home. Mike and I lived in Queens, and Ed lived out on Long Island. Ed hopped in the back seat, jammed up with all our camera equipment, and Mike took shotgun. Driving from

Manhattan to Queens after 2:00 a.m. is a joy with none of the ever-present New York traffic.

We made it to Mike's apartment quickly. With all our photography gear, we shifted everything around so Ed could get out of the backseat. We moved our gear next to the car as we reconfigured. After arranging everything over a lone city streetlight, Ed and I headed toward Suffolk County. Thirty minutes later, I dropped Ed off and headed back to my place in Queens at 4:00 a.m. I was dead tired and aching for my bed.

Pulling into the driveway, I sleepily opened the back door to get my camera equipment. It wasn't there. *It must be in the trunk,* I thought. Opening the trunk, I found nothing but my spare tire and a crowbar. I stared into the early morning sky as my heart raced.

Did Ed take my gear by accident? Did I leave it on the side of the street by Mike's apartment?

In the driver's seat seconds later, I zipped up 209th Street in Hollis with no concern about getting a ticket. All I could envision was my pile of camera equipment being taken from in front of his apartment. Two camera bodies. Three lenses. A flash and other accessories. I think I left $13,000 worth of gear on the side of the road.

I rounded the turn on Roosevelt Avenue not far from Shea Stadium. I pulled past the bodega where I often grabbed lunch, and a nervous calm came over me. I'm not far away. Almost there, I turned onto Mike's street, slowed down and started eyeballing the apartment numbers until I came close. I saw it in the distance, but it was dark. There was a tree right in front that hid the area.

I pulled up in the same exact spot where I parked two hours earlier. I jumped out, not even shutting off the car or closing my door. There it was, right in front of me. Nothing but grass and a tree.

The equipment was gone.

I regressed into a full-fledged panic. In complete denial, I opened all four car doors and the trunk, like all that gear could be hiding behind a door crack. It looked like a mafia hit gone wrong without the blood. Yelling out loud, I was beside myself.

I sprinted to the payphone at the corner in front of the bodega to call Ed to see if somehow he had mistakenly grabbed my stuff. He answered quickly, but he sounded so sad to tell me he hadn't. I fell silent. He asked if he should drive out to me, but I told him there was no point. Everything was gone.

Returning to my car and a little bit more clear with my thoughts, I saw that I left all my doors open with the keys in the ignition. Luckily, the same people didn't drive away in a car I was handing to them like my equipment. Inside the car, as a parting gift for me, was my 300mm lens. It was my most expensive lens, and for some reason it never left the car. Not by me or by someone walking by during those ten minutes of panic.

By now it was almost 6:00 a.m. The sun was rising, and I was spent. On the drive back home, I replayed those few minutes over and over in my head. How in the world did this happen? How did I do this? On top of it all, I had assignments to shoot the next day. Even more pressing was that I was heading to Ohio University for journalism school in a few months, and at this moment I didn't have any gear or the money to replace it.

I've always known that having insurance on my equipment was very important. Being self-employed, it was a necessity. It protected me from situations like this. That's why I had gotten the paperwork and filled them out months earlier. And after walking in the house early in the morning, there was the paperwork, sitting on top of my computer, having never been mailed out.

I dropped into bed with no equipment and no insurance. The savings I had set aside for college was now going towards a new set of photography equipment. I was left with nothing but a valuable lesson.

The Lone Wolf

So many of us strive to control our own destiny. I can't go a day without someone telling me how much he or she desires to leave their full-time, corporate job to go out and be a lone wolf. And as incredible as that life may seem, the experienced lone wolves have learned that there are downsides. Lone wolves tend to live in isolation. You might have a boss breathing over your neck right now, or a co-worker who chews their lunch next to you like a giraffe, and isolation sounds like the best thing ever. But isolation, over time, turns to loneliness. Loneliness can trigger overthinking, selfishness, depression, and anxiety. So, if you are going to become a lone wolf, you need to guard against the pitfalls.

The best way to accomplish that is to build your own personal wolf pack. The beauty of creating your own wolf pack is that you control who joins your pack. You aren't stuck spending time with the new hire who chomps on their gum all day, or your in-law who shoots down all your dreams. You get to systematically and methodically bring in those who are right for you while letting go of the ones who aren't.

The process will be one of the most rewarding—and necessary—parts of building your freelance life, but it's not easy. For starters, most people you know have full-time jobs. When you crave human interaction, which we all do, your best bet will be at Panera Bread next to all the senior citizens, at least if you don't have a wolf pack in place. No diss on the seniors—they seem to have more fun talking than the young people in there!—but finding, creating, and devoting time to your wolf pack adds tremendous value, even if it doesn't have to do with your business.

One way to accomplish this is to find friends and associates who desire this type of interaction as much as you do. It won't last long if you are into it much more than they are. Be selective of the people you let in because a warm body just won't do. You aren't looking for another drinking buddy. And if they are going to spend their time gossiping and complaining about life, you might wish for that time back. To make it work, schedule your time together weekly. Freelancers have irregular schedules, so don't worry about it being so structured on a date or time. Balancing a few of these relationships provides a sense of stability, community, and accountability that is deeply missing in the freelance world.

Speaking of accountability, using that word can take these relationships to an even greater level. I have my own personal "Accountability Club," where I depend on others to hold me accountable for the goals I set for myself—and I do the same for them. In creating an accountability club, you learn quickly who is serious and who is just looking to sip on a latte weekly. If your time is extra tight, or in-person meetings aren't possible with certain people, schedule by phone, Skype, or Zoom. These meetings are much more time-smart, but get some kind of weekly face-to-face meeting with someone in your wolf pack. No amount of internet connections replaces the feeling of an in-person get-together.

Another option is either forming, or joining, a mastermind group. Mastermind groups are growing rapidly in popularity but have been around since Ben Franklin and his famed Junto group. I now run and facilitate a handful of masterminds-based on living a life of financial, time and life freedom- and invest in another as well. Jim Rohn said that we are the average of the five people we spend the most time with. I've found this to be painfully true. When I spend time with underachievers, I also underachieve. When I spend time with complainers, I get better at complaining. Conversely, when I spend time with people who are looking to be better, looking to grow, looking to be challenged- I become that as well.

For the freelancer, the mastermind is vital. It brings together like-minded individuals with business, time, and family aspirations. Mastermind members should hold each other accountable, celebrate victories, and have difficult discussions when one of us isn't living up to their aspirations and who they wants to be.

I, too, thought I wanted to be a lone wolf, but creating my own wolf pack has added friendships, accountability, and a sense of community I could never have on my own.

Patience and Persistence

In 1998, I was a struggling twenty-six-year-old freelancer attempting to get my foot in the door to shoot for the Associated Press in New York City. Jonathan Elmer, the photo editor, was the man I needed to get in front of to show my work. I would call weekly—every Monday—to set up a time to meet. Each time we had a meeting scheduled, something would come up and he canceled.

He always seemed interested in talking with me, but could never find the time to get me in. Finally, after nearly six weeks of trying, I was invited to meet Jonathan in his office to show my portfolio.

After apologizing for making me jump through so many hoops to get to him, he said something that became the cornerstone in my mindset about becoming financially free.

"I want to thank you, Vincent," he said eloquently, "for your patience and your persistence. Without both, we wouldn't be here today."

I looked out his third-floor window at Rockefeller Center and filed away his comment in my mind while he looked through my photographs. In so few words, he managed to give me a mantra for life: patience and persistence. But when he mentioned that without both it wouldn't have happened, that was just as important.

Patience without persistence would have never gotten me in the door. Persistence without patience would have turned him off and turned me away. It was the right combination of patience and persistence that got me through his elusive door. I didn't know what I had done right until it was over. I only called once a week. I was patient. But I did call once a week, every week. I was persistent. When we took this lesson and put it toward chasing a life of time and money freedom, it took away all the guess work. Patience and persistence—it is the combination for success.

The Details

How thoroughly do you study the contracts you sign?

There is a story about the band Van Halen that has been elevated to rock n' roll lore since this rumor began in the 1980's. It was widely known that the band had included in their contract that there would be no brown M&M's in the backstage area of any arena where they performed. Even more onerous was that the contract stated that if there were brown M&M's found, the promoter would forfeit the entire show at full pay. Because of these ridiculous demands, the band was viewed as wildly eccentric and first-rate prima donnas.

But the truth behind the story is not so flamboyant, though it was certainly more practical. During this tour, Van Halen took what was, at the time, the largest production ever to hit the road. This massive set-up caused big problems because it was so cutting edge for its time. The giant lights, stage, and set-up were difficult to assemble in the older arenas. These venues often did not have loading docks with doorways that could conveniently accommodate the tour equipment.

The band noticed that the set-up for their shows was taking much longer to compete. The setup and tear-down times were going two to three times longer, and the cost of producing this tour skyrocketed due to union overtime costs. In addition to the stage crews in these different cities being unfamiliar with such a unique stage set, the band realized that the promoters were not reading the rider in the contract about the structural and electrical issues with the proper attention to detail. Even with the extra time, the set-up was in danger of an eventual structural collapse.

David Lee Roth, the flamboyant frontman of the band, came up with an idea. Just after a series of highly technical demands within the contract, Van Halen decided to put an odd, out-of-place requirement smack dab in the middle of the contract. That is where they selectively placed their goofy M&M request.

But it wasn't goofy at all. That one clause indicated to Roth and the band whether the production was done safely, or if there were issues to be addressed. If the band entered the backstage area and noticed brown M&M's mixed with the red, green, and blue, they knew the promoter did not read the contract rider. It would immediately set in motion a line check to make sure there were no danger issues in the stage or production—and a promoter being fired without pay.

The M&M request had nothing to do with egotistical rock stars who had nothing better to do except pick on people just because they can. It was a creative way of getting the attention of the people who controlled the safety of all the people involved at their shows.

The moral of the story? Read the contracts you sign. If not, you run the risk of harming people, losing your livelihood, and being stuck with nothing but a giant bag of M&M's, including the brown ones.

Why Do We Do What We Do?

Harry Chapin's song, Cat's in the Cradle, hits me in the heart every time I hear it. It's one of the rare songs that creates a flood of thoughts, emotions and feelings as soon as I hear the first few notes. I despise that song.

Actually, I love that song. I sing along every time I hear it. I despise the story behind it. If you aren't familiar with the Harry Chapin tune, it is a story about a dad who doesn't make time for his son while he is young. His son grows into a father, and their role switches and he becomes the son with no time for his dad. It's incredibly depressing and should serve as a warning to every parent today.

I heard the song driving home, and it made me somber but curious. I went home to look up stats about fathers today, and the results were even sadder than when the song was written in 1974.

- The average American father spends eight hours and forty-five minutes at work per day.
- The average American father watches two hours and forty-nine minutes of television per day.
- The average American father spends two hours and forty-two minutes on his phone.
- The average American father spends seven minutes a day talking with his children. I'm going to type that again just in case you might have missed it the first time. The average American father spends seven minutes a day talking with his children.

I heard a saying recently. I would have laughed if it wasn't so true. "Spend time with your kids now," it quipped, "or you will spend the time with them later in therapy."

I can't imagine that any father sets out to be part of these awful stats. When our first son, Andrew, was a baby, I know I watched more than three hours of television daily. It's difficult to admit how much time I wasted. But he was sleeping most of the time, so the endless reruns of Everybody Loves Raymond and The King of Queens weren't harming anybody, were they? And those Sundays watching football, football, and, oh, yeah, more football, were just my way of winding down.

It turns out that it's not about intentions, it's about habits. And I had developed some awful ones.

It wasn't until Dylan was born in 2011 that I began to pay attention to a nasty habit of mine. Our television was on constantly. It wasn't Elizabeth's idea, and the kids weren't big enough to turn it on. I guess that leaves me. The endless array of SportsCenter, mind-numbing sitcoms, or watching Dora the Explorer with the kids had me too distracted to pay attention.

In 2012, I got sucked into the political drama of the vitriolic presidential election between Barack Obama and Mitt Romney. As election night roared into the dramatic final hours, I heard Elizabeth upstairs playing a boisterous, belly-laugh-inducing game with the boys. I stared at the talking heads while they stirred the pot. When it became clear that Barack Obama was going to win, I heard a commentator excitedly mention how the race for 2016 would begin soon.

I turned off the television and realized immediately what a waste of time I had just allowed myself to get sucked into. It wasn't just that night—it was the months leading up to it. And they were now letting us all know that they would be fanning the flames for the next four years. I stared at the blank screen and realized that he would have been president the next day whether I watched the news or played with the kids. I had to think about the endless games on our television almost nightly. Is any baseball or hockey team worth three hours of my night?

As parents, we need to start asking ourselves a vital question.

What really matters?

It's obvious that work does matter. It provides fulfillment and income. We get to help others and provide a service that is valuable to them. But it no longer dictates our life or our time. Living in the freelance world like we have, every day can be a roller coaster of business emotions. I heard it said once that entrepreneurs are the only people who know what it feels like to go from extreme highs through excruciating lows on a daily basis. But it is just work. And it is just money.

We've decided, as a family, that what is on television doesn't matter. I'm proud to share that we cut the cable cord. Our evenings are filled with board games, horseplay, music, and awesome dinners by my wife. I still catch a football game many weekends, but I actually enjoy it more when it's on the radio. I can catch the game, spend time with the kids, and not be subjected to those horrendous commercials. I knew something had to change when our eight-year-old asked what erectile dysfunction was.

My next hurdle is my phone, which I'm having a more difficult time breaking up with. But it's important to be aware of its allure. When the television is off, it's out of my mind, but the phone is always there, enticing me with red alerts of new emails, Facebook comments, and an entire world of useless information. The email check disguises itself as a harmless little audit, but its circle of influence ensures that my attention is away from the people who matter.

These devices are a gift. They have made life much easier and more convenient in countless ways. But when the dad hat goes on, I need to be careful that it doesn't change from a gift to a sneaky, time-sucking diversion.

What matters—what truly matters—is our kids. I'm not talking about enabling them and giving them material things. I'm certainly not advocating making them believe that the earth revolves around their heads. I am talking about building healthy relationships within our family. Creating a strong bond to carry on through generations.

That can't be done by consistently putting in more overtime hours. It can't be done sitting in front of the television. It can't be done scrolling through an iPhone.

And it certainly can't be done in seven minutes.

Our kids will follow what we do, good or bad. And if we don't change as fathers, we are setting them up for failure. One of the final lines in Chapin's hit song describes the reality of what we, as dads, must come to grips with later if we don't change what we are doing now. The reality of becoming a father who wasn't there for his kid and raising a man who had grown up just like him.

Begin with the End in Mind

Stephen Covey, in his fantastic book *The 7 Habits of Highly Successful People*, wrote about beginning with the end in mind. I read Covey's book the year Nolan was born, and it was a catalyst in forging a plan for our life instead of allowing life to happen to us. As odd as it was to think about, Elizabeth and I sat down to write out what our ideal life would look like while raising our family. We went so far as to develop a plan for after they were grown. It allowed us to escape being consumed with the crisis of the month or the same old thinking that derailed us in the past. It was an opportunity to plan how we wanted to live, and then create a strategy to fulfill it.

When I was a kid, my mom told me and my brother that we were growing up too fast. I'd roll my eyes as fast as I'd wipe the lipstick off my cheek from her kiss, and then, even faster, I would run out the door to play with my friends. She was being dramatic, I told myself on my way to flip baseball cards or play football on our street. Now that we have three kids of our own, I can see that my mom was spot on. Time will not slow down for any of us, but what we do with that time is what matters. It's what we can control.

If you are a new parent, try for a moment to see beyond the sleepless nights you might be struggling with. For a moment, don't think about the constant feedings, diaper changes, or the dishes piling up in the sink. Try not to think about any of your struggles and thoughts about what needs to get done today. Instead, think about ten years from today. Sit down with your spouse and have what could become one of the most important conversations you could possibly have.

What do you want your life to look like ten years from today? For example, you might want three kids. Let's pretend they are similar in age to ours (eleven, nine, and five). Now envision that life. Do you both want to be working full-time for someone else? Would one of you want to stay at home? Can you envision having your kids in daycare, or would you want to be the one to spend that precious time with them? How much would you like to travel together? With the state of our public-school systems, is homeschooling something that sounds appealing? What kind of physical shape do you want to be in?

What about your friends? We learned the painful lesson that the friendships you had before children might not be as valuable, fun, or appealing once your kids start growing. Are your friends—and the children they might be raising—people you want to be around? They might be a riot to hang at the bar with, but will they be a good influence going forward?

What kind of house do you want to live in? The apartment you might be in right now is probably not ideal for a family of five, but is going deeply into debt for your dream home something you want around your neck as you raise your family? Or can you plan to have that house without jumping in headfirst and strapping your finances?

What is so sad witin our society today is how poorly we time our life purchases. We spend like crazy on cars, college, travel, and junk when we are very young— when it would be wise to prepare for our future. Once we collectively settle down with a family, we straddle ourselves with a huge mortgage, car payments, and credit card bills, then pile all those on top of our student-loan payments. No wonder parents are stressed out today! We slog through years of parenting while over-caffeinated, sleep-deprived, stressed out by money and our kids, and looking forward to the years ahead when things will be easier and less stressful.

And once the kids move out, we look around and wonder what happened. Where did that time go? There were so many things we planned to do together. There were so many trips we were going to take. So many days of fun that never happened. So much laughter and joy stripped away by the stresses of a self-induced busy life. Often, relationships never grow because work commitments, time-sucking activities like sports and gymnastics, and time on our phones steal that time away. And now they are gone.

If you think this kind of lifestyle doesn't affect the way your kids will see you when they are adults, think again. So, you wind up as a couple—if your marriage survived that tumultuous era —angry or depressed that you don't hear from your adult children. But, in actuality, it makes total sense. These kids were taught that a stressful, debt-filled, and time-starved adulthood is the norm. When you finally have the time again to breathe and money in your pockets again, your kids are following in your footsteps. Growing up in a stressed-out household takes an emotional toll on children. If you don't invest time into your children at a young age, you dramatically increase the chances of that relationship being damaged.

As you look toward the future, what life do you envision? And how can the work you do compliment the life you desire, as opposed to destroying it?

20 Questions

1. After Phase I, have you started a side business?
2. Do you agree with Marc Cuban's advice to the self-employed about taking out a loan to start a business?
3. Do you currently have debt on your business?
4. If so, how much?
5. Is there an area in your life where you are not "Owning It" right now?
6. What need are you risking for something that is not a need?
7. Does somebody else own you right now?
8. If so, who?
9. What are the tax advantages of being a small business owner instead of an employee?
10. Are you an entrepreneur or a freelancer?
11. Is there something you loved doing as a child that was squashed by an adult?
12. What are you doing right now, work-wise, that you don't want to do?
13. Do you say yes to too many requests?
14. Referring back to the Piano Man story, can you remember a time where you made the best of a bad work situation?
15. Do you have the proper insurance in all areas of your side business?
16. Can you recall a time when a giant struggle was turned into a big success?
17. If you have children, how much time, on average, do you spend with them each day?
18. Do you have a "wolf pack" you can count on?
19. Are you paying enough attention to the contracts you send out and sign?
20. What do you want your life to look like ten years from today?

PHASE III

THE OPTIMIZED FREELANCER

A t the beginning of Phase III, your life is on an upward path. If you were a stock, I'd be looking to buy. You are getting it together. You've started a side business and dealt with the initial growing pains involved. You are learning from your mistakes and ready to grow.

If things are on track, you are bringing in more than 50% of the income you need to live from that business. If that is the case, you might still be at your full-time job. Or if you are riskier (or have been laid off), you are already gone. But leaving is getting closer, and you can feel it. If you are following the plan outlined in this book, you are paying down your debt with your business income. You've researched all your investment options. You have the insurance you need to protect you from danger.

Your family life is also in a better place. You are more attentive with your family. The stress and drama you have felt is beginning to fade. There is still much work to be done, but you are more energized than anxious. You start to see the future in a positive light for a change, and you start to realize that with more money freedom, you will soon get more mental freedom. With mental freedom comes new ideas, which is how you move to more time, money, and life freedom. But let's not get too far ahead of ourselves. Let's learn from Phase III.

Be Better than Yesterday

Focusing simply on being better than yesterday was the single factor that showed me how to have consistent progress and not get overwhelmed. It also showed me how not to become complacent. It has been such a fine line to get that mindset working. If my mind goes to the future, I become overwhelmed. Nothing will be good enough, and I feel as if I'm moving too slow. If I become too satisfied, I become complacent, and nothing seems urgent. I'm happier during this time because not much stresses me out, but it catches up if it goes on too long. 'Better than yesterday' does for my mind, body, and soul what tuning does for my guitar.

Do you ever get overwhelmed by everything on your plate? Join the club. You are not alone. Overwhelmed is common in the freelance world. What do I do first? How do I handle everything coming my way at such a rapid pace? How do I juggle family, business, health, money, and relationships?

I was constantly overwhelmed. I would look into the future and worry. I would fret about money. I'd stress myself out over what might happen with our business. I'd fall out of touch with friends.

I'd be concerned about our kids and family. I'd think back in anger at things that actually did happen. These thoughts would constantly keep me up at night and wake me early in the morning.

I woke up early fretting over today, tomorrow, and forty years from now. I asked myself how in the world can I handle all this? There was always something to worry about, even on the most beautiful days. This, I was sure, was no way to live.

After more than enough quiet mornings staring at the ceiling, four words came into my head while I laid in the darkness of our bedroom.

Be better than yesterday.

That's all I need to do. If I followed my own advice, all I needed to think about was today. How can I improve from the day before?

I didn't need to lose twenty-five pounds; I just need to do better than yesterday in my food choices.

I didn't need to make a certain amount of money this year; I just need to reach out and connect with one new person.

I didn't need to scour the internet for networking get-togethers; I just need to send one encouraging, unexpected email to someone I already know who I've lost touch with.

I didn't need to figure out everything bothering my son; I just need to go for a walk with him and listen.

I didn't need to overhaul our website; I just need to add one new photograph to it.

I didn't need to schedule a long-needed vacation with my wife; I just need to give her more attention today.

I didn't need to spend hours learning about SEO; I just need to publish a blog post for the first time in a month.

'Better than yesterday' gave me the freedom to push the past aside, stop worrying about the future, and concentrate on what needs to be done today. Because nothing else matters besides today. Have you ever seen tomorrow? I don't think I have.

Every day of my life has been today. Not yesterday or tomorrow; not the past or the future. It's just today. And if you make today better than yesterday, the past will be quickly forgotten and the future will become incredibly bright.

Don't Give Yourself a Bad Assignment

Marcy Nighswander was one of my professors at the School of Visual Communications at Ohio University. Nighswander is a no-nonsense, tell-it-like-it-is type of teacher. The former Associated Press staff photographer won the Pulitzer

Prize in 1991 for her compelling photograph during the presidential debate. In one image, she perfectly illustrated the personalities of each candidate. Bill Clinton was poised and in command, George H.W. Bush seemed a bit out of touch, and H. Ross Perot was just goofy. It was the perfect frame at the perfect moment.

Nighswander commanded the attention of the classroom, as well. She possessed a witty sense of humor, but had the respect of her students. She never lost control of the classroom. The lessons she taught were always to the point, poignant, and at times, biting. Marcy threw around compliments like she threw around manhole covers. So, if she said you did well, there was the assured satisfaction that you actually did well.

Emphasizing personal responsibility, Nighswander routinely gave us the flexibility to find the photo assignments we were passionate about and eager to develop. And when one of us turned a great opportunity into a lame project, she was waiting there, noose and all.

"You had the opportunity to choose any assignment your heart desired, and you chose this?" she questioned one of my classmates. When the student stared blankly ahead without an answer, Marcy doled out some serious life advice disguised as a photo tip.

"Don't give yourself a bad assignment," she pronounced.

That twenty-year-old student reacted to her statement as I might at his age. But I didn't go back to get my degree until I was twenty-six, so her words struck me differently. I had already given myself tons of bad assignments in life. That job dressed as Santa Claus years back. Yeah, I gave myself that one. Staying in a dead-end convenience store job for five years? Nobody came to my house begging me to work there. I signed up for that one all by myself. In fact, I signed up for all of them. That is, until I replaced 'assignment' with words like life, friends, and experiences.

Life doesn't usually happen to us—we happen to life. We get to decide the places we work and the people who surround us. We choose those assignments. I think it's important for you to give yourself a moment to think about the assignments you have given yourself. What can you learn from them? What assignments are you giving yourself now? Are they good assignments?

Your life is open-ended—not much different than the photo assignments we were given back at Ohio University. It's your choice whether you turn it into a great opportunity or a lame project. Contrary to what the news, your broke brother-in-law, or the naysayers in your life may say, you get to choose your shots. If you have a history of choosing bad assignments for yourself, you've got added work to do. But you still get to choose your own shots.

Every decision in life is an assignment you give yourself. One of the first steps out is to stop giving yourself bad assignments. What assignment will you give yourself tonight? Will it be one that includes downing a bottle of wine while staring at the television? Or one that grows a relationship, a business, or your health?

You give yourself the assignments of your life.

Do the Opposite

I hardly watch television anymore. This isn't a proud, boastful, or high-and-mighty statement. There are just so many things I want to do more. There was a time, though, when I watched more television than I would like to admit. Most of it was mindless, relatively harmless entertainment.

But every once in a while there was a morsel of wisdom that came through the tube.

Often, it came from *Seinfeld*. One episode, called *The Opposite,* made me laugh as much as it made me think.

George Costanza, Jerry's neurotic, self-absorbed friend, sat in a diner lamenting about what went wrong with his life. How it once held so much promise.

"It all became very clear to me today that every decision that I've ever made in my entire life has been wrong," Costanza said sadly. "My life is the complete opposite of everything I want it to be."

He then starts to order lunch, realizing he always orders the same thing. In frustration, George decides to switch it up and order the opposite of what he usually gets. Right afterwards, Elaine points out to George that an attractive woman just looked his way and suggests he go talk to her.

"Elaine," George explains with emphasis, "bald men with no jobs and no money, who live with their parents, don't approach strange women."

"Well, here's your chance to try the opposite," Jerry chimes in. "If every instinct you have is wrong, then the opposite would have to be right."

A look of conviction appeared on George's face. Costanza built up the nerve to walk up to the blond woman at the counter.

"My name is George," he says nervously, "I'm unemployed, and I live with my parents."

The woman turns toward George with a look of intrigued interest. "I'm Victoria," she says provocatively. "Hi...."

Raise your hand if there is an area of your life where you need to do the opposite. I'll go first.

I have a tendency to work on what I am good at. Just slightly. Well, maybe compulsively. I'll get up and get started on my strengths. For instance, I write best first thing in the morning. So, for the past few months, naturally, I got up and wrote. But what I do best doesn't always mean it's the best for me. If you asked me what area of my life I need to pay more attention to, it would be my relationships. If I were honest ten years ago, the answer would have been the same. I would have flicked that thought away, explaining that I needed to work to provide an income for my family.

I recently watched *The Opposite* clip again, and knew that I needed to funnel my inner George Costanza.

It took me too long to realize I can't keep doing the same thing and expecting different results.

What exactly is the point of success, freedom, and money without healthy, great, intimate friendships? It's so easy to become focused on our own lives, struggles, and obstacles that we lose sight of what others are going through.

I don't naturally wake up and think, "What can I do directly to make someone else better?"

That's a tough thing to write. Now you might be much better at this than I am, and I hope you are. But the thing I needed to improve more than anything was the same one I always put on the back burner.

Now growing, investing in, and nurturing my friendships and relationships became where I did the opposite.

What about you? Where do you need to do the opposite?

Look around. 50% of Americans have no savings and would have to go into debt to pay for an unexpected $500 expense. The majority of workers are unhappy with their jobs. Nearly 75% of men are overweight and almost 40% are obese. 50% of marriages end in divorce. Doing something blindly because you always have, or because everyone else is, is a recipe for pain and heartache. If you are doing what everyone is doing, you are going to get what everyone is getting.

Be like George. Do the opposite.

The Hour of Giving

As part of doing the opposite, instead of working on business when I begin work, most days I start "The Hour of Giving". It was inspired by something my wife said in a conversation with one of our sons. He was picking on his brother, and Elizabeth explained to him that whatever type of energy he puts out into the world, that's what will come back to him. I saw his response, and how well he received her message.

I asked myself the same question. What kind of energy am I putting out? I thought about my friendships and the people who have helped me, directly or indirectly.

Was I putting great energy into their lives? Was I thinking about how I could help them? Aside from my closest friends and my family, what was I doing to make other people's lives better? I wasn't happy with my answers, so "The Hour of Giving" was born.

The Hour of Giving is simple, yet life-changing. We all crave positive energy in our lives, so I dedicate the first working hour of my morning to writing reviews for the books and podcasts I love. I promote my friends' services and businesses. I write handwritten thank-you notes to people in my life I appreciate. I go through social media and affirm the people in my life.

The only problem with The Hour of Giving is that it's so much fun and so rewarding, it's hard to do it all in an hour. I can see this creeping into "The Hours of Giving."

Let me ask you something. When was the last time you received an unexpected, handwritten note? Are you ready for a tougher question? When was the last time you sent one?

If you are looking for one area of your life that will improve all the other areas of your life, create your own "Hour of Giving."

The energy you put out into the world will indeed be the energy you get back from it.

The Power of No

"The difference between the successful people and the very successful people is that the very successful people say 'no' to almost everything."
—**Warren Buffett**

There comes a time as a freelancer when you need to learn to say no. For such a tiny word, it was hard for me to say.

At first, we said yes to everything. Everything! Often with a new business, your first clients are friends. So, not only do you want to help them, but you could use the work. But mixing business with friendship can hurt your business and ruin your friendships if you don't create solid and clear boundaries early and often.

Saying no is hard, but it doesn't mean you have to be a jerk. Sometimes a job is tempting. Being able to say no is so much more important than being able to say yes, however. Here are just a few of the requests we've said no to, and the responses we gave to lighten the situation while remaining firm.

(From a friend) "I should just have you take my portrait. The professionals we looked at are expensive."

Ouch.

My sister is getting married, I told her you would shoot it!"

Would you like us to send her our price list first?

"Can I get the friend discount?"

It's been a really long time since we've talked! How have you been all these years?

"Oh, you can just Photoshop that out later."

It's probably quicker for all of us if we just moved the purse out of the way now.

"Since you are coming to the party anyway, can you bring your camera?"

Thank you, but I'd love to enjoy the party like everyone else invited!

"The other photographers' prices are much cheaper. Can you match their price?"

That sounds like a great deal you're getting. You should hire them right away!

"But we love your work so much. It's so much better than theirs."

Yeah, that's probably why they are so much cheaper.

"It will only take a few minutes."

We've learned from experience that nothing only takes a few minutes. I've attached our minimum rate for you.

"We have a very small budget, but we want great pictures."

Thank you for your interest! Our rates start at…

"Can you photograph my son's wedding as your gift?"

We don't normally give a $5,000 gift for a wedding. But can you send us their registry?

"Make sure I don't look fat!"

I made the mistake once of saying "I'm a photographer, not a magician." I'm still working on a better response.

It can be good for the soul to say no. It has often led us to booking a better, nicer client. Saying no early and often will give you more time, higher rates, and better friends.

Morning JEM

"The great thing about the future is that it comes at us one day at a time."— **Abraham Lincoln**

Time freedom has its obstacles. When I worked for someone else, my time was scheduled for me. I had tasks to think about, but little free time to think about deeper ideas. When I got home at night, I didn't want to think about anything but what was on TV and what beer was in the fridge. Once we got out of the rat race, it was glorious. At first. The first few years of being in control of our time felt like what a prisoner must feel after they are released from prison. But there are perils to too much free time, and I fell victim. I want to help you avoid what I experienced.

Like a slow drip, my mindset began to change for the worse. It took a few years for it to really take shape. Instead of feeling grateful for the wonderful life we had, I began to worry about the future. Instead of living in the present, I got lost on mental rabbit trails. Without the pressing need to earn income daily, I became complacent. All these thoughts and habits led to an uneasy feeling I couldn't shake. I used to wake up in the morning excited for the upcoming day. Aside from planning for the future, I was fully engaged in that day alone. But then I started waking up and looking past that day. My thoughts immediately turned to the future.

And the future can be a crazy place if you let it. Every possible scenario is on the table and rife for worry. Not only for my own life, but for my wife and kids. Each morning, the future is directly where my mind went. And after enough worry and sleep-deprived nights, I was struck with anxiety. Being as free as I was, I had plenty of time to worry! Instead of having to go to an office, or deal with a commute, I was free to lay in my bed and put myself into a mental panic. I had everything I ever wanted in life, and yet I chose to make myself miserable. Each day became a bleary-eyed chore, something I needed to get through instead of enjoy. I tried to put on a good face around our children, who were having too much fun to see my pain. At least I hoped they couldn't see it.

My sleep was down to just a few fragmented hours a night, and I woke up nightly with a racing heart. The lack of sleep just exasperated my issues. With my drive to work vanquished, I became the epitome of a man going through the motions. After a few months, I needed to finally admit that I had a big problem on my hands.

Actually, it was a big problem in my mind. Anxiety was the new subject I was now forced to study. I searched websites, forums, and books about the subject while my wife and kids slept soundly upstairs. Having never experienced this before, I was surprised at how common it is— and there was no shortage of advice being doled out for me to take in. The recovery was like being on a see-saw. No, it was actually more like a roller coaster. I would implement some of the suggestions, and they would work wonderfully for a few days before my old habits set back in. Three great days would be followed by four days in a funk.

Why was this such a crazy thing to shake? On my good days, the future looked incredibly bright. I was excited and motivated. The deep engagement with Elizabeth and the boys was back. My ideas flowed, and each day was a blessing. And before I knew what happened, I went back to hell. The pattern was always the same. It would start with negative thoughts. The night would end with these thoughts in my mind, and then the next few days became a blur of sadness, depression, and hopelessness. I didn't understand why these days got so bad, and I couldn't remember how to feel good again, until I asked myself how the good days got so good. That's when I finally got back on the right path. There were three practices I did sporadically throughout this long episode, though I didn't stick with them consistently. I eventually named it my "Morning JEM", and it is the process that got me back and better than ever.

JEM stands for Journaling, Exercise and Meditation.

Journaling

One of the recurring suggestions of the happiest people I studied was their habit of keeping a journal. I had never journaled a day in my life. To see the positive, I decided to start writing down the good things that happened that day. I noticed quickly that there were a lot of good things to write about, even on the bad days. I kept up that habit for three weeks straight before missing a few days. Around that time, the anxiety and negative thoughts crept back in. Once that happened, I lost the desire to journal more. I'd look at the book, shake my head, and walk past.

Three weeks later, I forced myself to pick it up again. I felt guilty for falling off and not recording those days on paper. Even though I was in a funk, we had some great times I should have written down. This juggling act went on for months before it finally got through my thick head.

Journaling has tremendous benefits besides writing down all the things happening in our lives. When I journaled, I thought only of that day. I thought less about the future, and that led to a more peaceful mindset. When I didn't journal—especially in the fragile state of mind I was in— I slipped back into future thinking and not be present.

Journaling changed the way I thought about each day. Instead of thinking days, weeks, and years ahead, I needed to be present because I needed to write down what I did that day. It held me accountable to not only where my mind goes, but where my day goes. And being self-employed, it's imperative we have something to hold us accountable. But there was an even greater benefit from journaling—I noticed I would go out of my way to do something helpful because I wanted to write it down in the journal. Instead of saying, "In a few minutes" when one of the kids asked to play a game, like I had fallen into the trap of doing, I immediately said, "Yes." I honestly felt like doing some more fretting, but I was accountable to the journal. We would have a great time, my mind would get away from the anxiety, and I had another positive thing to put into the journal.

After a few more slip-ups when I forgot to journal—and the subsequent malaise that occurred on those days—I knew I had to make this a daily practice. Not only did it change my mindset, increase happiness, and reduce anxiety, I now had a written history of all the things occurring in our life on a daily basis. I will occasionally flip through the journal and read entries from months past and delight in the little moments I had written down. Funny sayings by the boys, jokes, and experiences that would have long been forgotten. Knowing they were remembered and recorded feels so valuable. My only regret is that I didn't start sooner.

Exercise

Nothing brightens up the start of my day like a good workout. And you don't have to lift weights to lift your spirits. Simply taking a twenty-minute stroll in the morning with sunshine beating down on your face can dramatically improve your mood, outlook, and positivity. The increased oxygen supply and proper circulation increases your brain power, leads to an enhancement of mental alertness, and increases your memory. According to a study from the Harvard Medical School, patients suffering from depression had a significant improvement in their condition by walking fast 35-60 minutes a day.

Why does sunlight matter? The sun's first rays are vital for absorbing Vitamin D—and a lack of Vitamin D has been linked to increased depression. In a study of more than 31,000 participants, researchers at the Department of Psychiatry and Behavioral Neurosciences, St Joseph's Hospital, Hamilton, Ontario, Canada, found a strong correlation between the lack of Vitamin D and depression.

Meditation

For years, Elizabeth attempted to get me to try meditation. I brushed it off, explaining flippantly that it wasn't for me. Everyone is wired differently, I rationalized, and my personality is one of high energy. I took the mood swings that came with that higher energy as collateral damage. I'd take the lows that went with the wonderful highs brought on by my drive, ambition, and personality. That was easy for me to say, she must have thought, because I don't have to live with me. I tried yoga classes with her a few times, but it was a painful experience. Not physically, but mentally. I felt it was a complete waste of time. I've got things to do, my mind is racing with ideas, and these people were doing nothing but breathing deeply for an hour? Not for me.

When I finally hit bottom that dark winter, I looked into breathing techniques. Of course, I still wouldn't admit I was meditating. To me, it had a stigma associated with kookiness. I agreed that I did feel calmer when I tried it, but I wouldn't allow myself to relax enough to get optimal results. Each time I tried it, I was ready to stop. Elizabeth continued to encourage me, knowing that this could create a radically positive shift in my life.

As I did more research, my skepticism dissipated. While on a late-night information binge brought on by another sleepless night, I came across a revolutionary study by the Massachusetts General Hospital and Harvard University. This extensive study determined that eight weeks of daily meditation for thirty minutes helped participants experience lower anxiety, greater feelings of calm, and growth in the areas of the brain associated with empathy, sense of self, stress regulation, and memory. The more we strengthen our brains in times of low stress, it explained, the more our brains respond positively during times of heightened stress.

And so it began. I set aside the twenty-seven minutes doctors recommend and got uncomfortable. Walking on fire might be less painful for an always-talking, constantly thinking native New Yorker than sitting still in complete silence for almost a half hour.

It wasn't difficult at first—it was torture. I had no idea my mind was so filled with chatter. Instead of thinking about my breathing, I was thinking about what I wanted to eat for lunch. It would quickly move toward an email I forgot to send, and then toward some story I read on the internet that annoyed me.

Often, my meditation lasted less than three minutes before I quit. I began to worry that I would never be able to quiet my mind. But over time, it got easier. One morning, a month later, I closed my eyes and concentrated on my breath. In what felt like an instant, I opened them twenty minutes later. I felt a calm within myself that was reserved only for quiet moments during a beach vacation.

Six months later, it became a habit. Along with the twice-daily habit came an entirely new sense of self-awareness. I noticed my impatience with our children instead of brushing it off. I could see how a difficult business decision increased my heart rate. Instead of reacting, I now take a series of deep breaths. It is still a work in progress, but the benefits are astounding.

It turns out the rumors were false. You can teach an old dog new tricks.

Go Make Something Better

One struggle with starting your own business is that somebody is already doing it.

We all have ideas, but unfortunately, just about every one of them is squashed in our mind before even saying the idea out loud. There's already a pizza place, or a gym, or that online course. There are already people building apps, becoming personal trainers, or starting dog-walking businesses. It's already been done. And if you don't say it, a relative or friend will. The world doesn't need another coffee shop.

But what does the world need? If you can answer that question and create a way to solve it, you're in business.

That does not mean it has to be a new idea. It can be the same idea, just better. It's easier to make an existing idea better than it is to build an entirely new market. Look around your office and notice something. Your lamp. The one you bought wasn't from the inventor. It was from someone who made it better. Your computer. Your desk. Your chair. All done better. And if you bought something that wasn't done better—most likely because it was cheaper—you will notice that, too.

When we started in wedding photography, it was sobering to see there were wedding photographers everywhere. How in the world do you stand out in an oversaturated market? In journalism school, we were taught the structure of a story. It was only natural to us that wedding photography should be a story.

I spent hours each day going through the websites of as many local wedding photographers as possible. What stood out like a blurry, out-of-focus photograph was that wedding photographers collectively started shooting a little before the ceremony began and wrapped up shortly after the formal dances concluded. In the wedding world, that was normal. But as an outsider from the photojournalism world, there was a big, gaping hole crying out for attention. Elizabeth went out and found a wedding to shoot for free—the day before she ran in a half marathon—and shot it from start to finish. That wedding, along with some pictures we made at various friends' weddings, comprised our first website.

In an oversaturated market, where local photographers told us there was no business, we booked twenty-five weddings in our first year using primarily word-of-mouth marketing. We had secured almost as much money in bookings from a self-created, rinky-dink website filled with not one photograph we were paid to shoot, as both our full-time jobs put together. We didn't create a new market. We saw a need to be filled, and we filled it. So did Starbucks. And Trader Joe's. And Air BnB. And all the small businesses that dot the landscape of your town.

So can you. Go make something better.

And if you want to know why Elizabeth, and not I, shot that wedding while she was getting ready to run a marathon, I have a perfectly good answer.

I was just wondering the same thing.

Choices

For the first time in the history of man, we actually have too many items to choose from. There are more than 127 flavors of Coca-Cola and more websites than people. There are 300 hours of content uploaded to YouTube each minute. On average, Americans get 189 cable television channels. But we still only get two choices for the president of the United States. (Insert biased political joke here.)

As you grow your self-employed venture, your greatest obstacle will not be your competition. It will not be government regulations. It's not the internet, robots coming to take your job, or some hack starting a side business undercutting you on the cheap.

Your greatest obstacle will be distraction.

Your phone. Texting. Snapchat filters, or whatever the flavor of the day is by the time you read this.

A recent study revealed that it takes eighteen minutes to get back on track after being distracted by a text or email. That means that we're pretty much distracted all the time. Now, for the rest of the knuckleheads that wander around earth walking into buildings while looking at their phones, that's fine. But not for you. You will not allow distractions to derail you from your purpose in life. Right?? Wait, did you get that? Oh, you got a text? Are you back now? Wow, was that really eighteen minutes?

Oh, yeah, I'm sorry, where were we? I forgot. We were talking about distractions or something.

Readers Lead

It was one of those loud, neighborhood days. Myself and a few friends tossed the football around, trying to get a few more recruits to start up a game. Across the street, a neighbor and a group of her friends played around on her lawn, listening to music and talking loud enough for all of us to hear. Sitting on our porch, with his back to the front door, my brother sat alone with a book in his hands. Blocking out the sounds that would have caused me to close the book and run out to play,

Steve was tuned in so intensely that the loud, teenage sounds didn't even challenge to his focus.

Tony, the boyfriend of our neighbor, noticed my brother sitting alone. I was on our front lawn getting ready to toss the football when I looked back to watch the exchange. He approached Steve quizzically, kind of like a little kid approaches a strange bug.

"Yo, Steve," he said in his heavy Brooklyn accent, "waddaya doin'?"

Deeply caught up in the book, Steve snapped his head up after a brief delay. "I'm reading," Steve said matter-of-factly. He noticed that Tony looked confused, so he waited for a response.

"Why?" Tony blurted out.

Silence followed. Steve eventually picked the book back up and began reading again. Tony headed back to the afternoon party on the neighbor's lawn. I held on to the football for a few extra seconds, thinking about what I just heard. Why? Did he really ask why he was reading a book? It wasn't a, 'for what particular reason are you reading this specific book' question. It was a 'why would you even read a book' type of question.

I don't know whatever happened to Tony. But that question hung with me long after I eventually tossed the football back to my friend. I don't believe I have ever asked someone why they would read a book, but I certainly wasn't someone who would be asked that question either, because I didn't read books. When I read, it was Sports Illustrated. Maybe that's why I started to feel as dumb as Tony sounded. I began paying attention to my brother's conversations a little more. I quickly realized how much he added to dialogues based on what he read. I stood by quietly during those conversations, only adding a sarcastic, barely witty comment to draw a little attention to myself.

According to the Statistic Brain Research Institute, 33% of high-school students will not read a book for the rest of their lives. Even more shocking, 42% of college graduates never read another book after college. Only one in seven of this year's graduating college students will read a book this year.

The one single, dominating factor in how we brought our businesses from start-up to successful are the books we read (I've highlighted a few throughout this book as an homage). If I had been left alone with my thoughts, I would still be at that dead-end convenience-store job selling Twinkies. If I didn't already get fired.

Books—specifically non-fiction, personal-development books—changed my life for the better in every way.

What Can I Do to Help?

Can you change your life with one question? I believe you can. We were able to change dinner-time at our house with one simple question. Our three boys are awesome, but kids naturally aren't thinking of others. They are pretty hedonistic, to borrow a line from Dr. Kevin Leman, one of our parental mentors. Each night, as Elizabeth put the finishing touches on our meal, each child would come into the kitchen and ask the same question.

"What are we having for dinner?" It wasn't out of excitement—it was more out of negotiation. One of them was primed to complain or try to bargain for something different to eat. And one night, Elizabeth had enough.

"Every night, you want to know what's for dinner. How come nobody asks what can they do to help?"

These mini-people didn't know how to respond. They each flashed a confused look that showed they always thought we were only here to serve them.

"Nobody is allowed to ask what's for dinner any more until they ask what they can do to help first," Elizabeth declared. They were still confused.

"But," Nolan said quietly, "what's for dinner?" He didn't get an answer.

"What can I do to help?" he responded quickly, eyes now widened.

With that one question, the dinnertime experience had been transformed. Oh, it took a while for it to cement itself. There are many nights when the old habits return, but 'What can I do to help' has now been ingrained into each of their heads. Meal times are no longer a time when they saunter over to be served like a king. It is now a time for cooperation, teamwork, and helpfulness. Our self-seeking offspring are learning the benefits of thinking of someone else first. They have even been caught battling for the opportunity to set the table.

Almost anything in life can have a lesson that relates to business or family. It's instinctual for all of us to look out for what's in it for us—even more so when we are just starting out. But what if, instead of asking what you're getting, you change that question. What if the first thing you ask is, "What can I do to help?"

How would you be perceived by your clients? How much more trust would you build? How much could the word-of-mouth marketing of your business spread if you had the mindset of looking for a way to help first? You might say that you already do this, but do you really?

I study small businesses, and I look for this mindset. It's been disappointing to see how often this question is never asked, and if it is, it is done in a manner that doesn't reflect a genuine heart. The least successful small businesses are run with a selfish and scarce mindset. Have you ever done more business with someone simply because you liked them, even when you didn't need it? On the flip side, have you ever walked away from a transaction with a bad feeling, even if the product was good? This happens to me all the time.

Practice asking that one question over and over again—"What can I do to help?" Not only will your customers be thrilled to give you their business, you will amaze yourself with the ideas and products you come up with.

Fear and Pain

Pain can be a fantastic motivator. It can also be a debilitating albatross. In Part I, I told the story of my father's struggle to dig himself out of a huge financial mess that nearly crushed our family. The fear I felt from that experience turned out to be an enormous advantage in my life.

If that situation would have happened when I was a few years older, it wouldn't have had the same impact. I wouldn't have felt the pain the same way. But that pain gave me the understanding to tell my fifteen-year-old self that I never wanted my kids to feel the way I was feeling, or for me as a father to go through what my dad had to deal with.

Although I coasted through my twenties as a financial illiterate, the pain of that teenage experience was felt from within once Elizabeth and I began to have thoughts about starting a family. It gave me the drive to dive in, study, and master a subject that I had never given much thought to.

I would never go so far as saying that fear is a positive emotion. I would much rather you learn the lesson without feeling the pain. But pain is inevitable. How we respond to the pain will define our lives more than the temporary discomfort we deal with in that moment.

I am confident that if my teenage years were smooth sailing, I would have had little to no interest in mastering the topic of money and how it relates to families. I wouldn't have had the slightest perspective of how important it was to teach our children that lesson.

So how do you use fear and pain?

Do you allow it to stop you in your tracks?

What fear do you have that can be used to become your greatest advantage?

What pain have you experienced in your life that you can turn on its ear and make someone else's life better?

Pain can crush you or it can drive you. The beauty is, you get to choose the answer.

The Pain of Opportunity

Oftentimes, our greatest successes rise from our greatest struggles.

Fifteen years after the *Seinfeld* incident, the lessons hadn't stopped. I'm assured now that they never will. The feeling that day is hard to forget. Because of a bulging disc in my back, I was in the most physical pain I had ever felt. Inflammation caused my left leg and lower back to shut down as the nerves screamed at me with each move I made. Everything was painful, including sitting, sleeping, and obviously, walking.

Elizabeth and I shot a wedding the night before, with Elizabeth taking over everything. I was there physically, but was useless after a few minutes of working. It was the only time in my life I could not work through pain. After three or four steps, the pain became so severe that it felt like my muscles might explode.

Compounding this, I was scheduled to photograph a Pittsburgh Penguins hockey game for a prominent outlet the following afternoon. The game was at noon. Elizabeth and I left the wedding at 1:00 a.m. as she pleaded with me not to shoot the game. This was only my second assignment for this company, which I had been trying to get into for more than a year.

"I can't say no," I explained. "They won't call me back again if I back out last-minute."

When we got home, I put the camera batteries on the charger before dropping into bed. Like most of those nights, sleep was painful and sporadic. I didn't sleep more than two hours before the alarm went off. With the pain no different than the night before, I haphazardly packed my gear and limped to the car.

Every step was a challenge. On my way into the arena, I stopped after ten steps just to catch my breath and let the pain subside. This continued all the way to the photo area, where, in a cold sweat, I needed a few minutes to sit and deal with the pain. Hockey, unlike football, is not a physical sport to photograph. The only walking involved is moving to your photo position from where we transmit our images. That would be a challenge, but I could take my time doing it.

I opened my case an hour before the puck dropped and stared at my bag in disbelief.

With the pain and lack of sleep, I managed to leave my batteries sitting on the charger at home. As I picked up the cameras in shock, I also discovered that I took a broken camera that was to be sent in for repair. Not wanting the other photographers to sense my panic, I walked into the hallway to call Elizabeth to see if she could swing by to drop off batteries and a camera.

That's when we realized that I took the vehicle with the kids' car seats in them. Wanting to scream, I hung up and did my best to remain calm. My only option was to borrow a battery that fit my Nikon camera from another photographer.

The warm-ups were beginning, and the ten photographers shooting the game exited to go shoot. I sat alone, stunned. If I didn't figure this out in a few minutes, I was screwed. The pain was so severe that I couldn't think straight. I'd never done anything like this before. Being so tired when I left, and in so much pain, I made a series of stupid mistakes that were about to cost me dearly. How could I explain that I was here, but had no way to shoot the game?

Joe Sargent, the Pittsburgh Penguins team photographer, walked in. Knowing Joe used Nikon, I did my best to not sound desperate. Asking if he had an extra battery, he informed me that he did and got one for me. He then left to go shoot some more pictures of the team. I then noticed the battery didn't include the special clip to keep it in place. I had to figure out something. I inserted the battery and held it firmly, using my fingers in place of the clip, and watched the power come on. I released the pressure, and it shut off. I realized all I needed was tape to keep it in place. I generally keep duct tape in my large bag, but the bag I had was a simple transport bag with just a few supplies.

I was close, but still not there. Looking through my side pockets, I found a small roll of scotch tape. I figured it was worth a shot, thinking there was no way it would hold. To my amazement, it worked. The camera turned on, and I was back in business. Now dragging my leg, I made it to my photo position right before the game started.

The game was a struggle. I needed to twist my body from my photo position to get the images I needed, which caused more pain in my back and legs. It prevented me from getting many of the images I was hoping for. I was able to re-tape the battery in between periods to avoid disaster. Walking back and forth between periods became more difficult. By the time the second period ended, I questioned if I could even make it back to transmit. I was so slow in getting back that half of the photographers had already returned, finished their edits, and were headed back out to the ice by the time I even entered the room. I tried to conceal the pain, but it was obvious something was wrong by the muffled grunts I emitted.

I was so far behind that I didn't make it out to the ice for the third period until there were twelve minutes left. The Penguins took the lead in the third and beat the Boston Bruins 3-2.

Somehow, I had captured the key goals.

Under normal circumstances, I would have run back to send the remaining images as fast as possible, but being in so much pain, I decided to let the crowd file out before I stood up. After the game ended, the three stars of the game are announced and the players return to the ice for acknowledgement. I was in position, so I decided to shoot a few images of those moments. It looks different than the game because they shut all the house lights down and put a spotlight on the players.

The first star of the game was Sidney Crosby, the Penguins superstar, who lifted his stick toward the crowd and happened to spin right in my direction. I shot that last image and hobbled slowly back. There was no rush now. The hard part was done. I transmitted my images from the now empty photo room. Having sent all the game images, the last shot I sent was the one of Crosby.

The following week, the road to recovery began as I made improvements with my diet, physical therapy, and tons of stretching. Around two months later, the pain was nearly gone. Seven months of intense, debilitating pain finally became a thing of the past. I was able to play with our kids outside and work full days without thinking about it.

On a random afternoon, while playing hockey in the back yard with our boys, I received an email titled "Congrats". It took a few moments for it to sink in that my colleague, Bruce Bennett, was informing me Sports Illustrated had selected a photograph of mine for a two-page spread in their latest issue. I couldn't believe my eyes! That had been a major goal of mine since I started shooting sports eighteen years earlier.

I emailed back to thank him and ask which photograph they used. He copied a screenshot of the page and sent it back to me to reveal Sidney Crosby spinning at the end of the Bruins game.

Throughout all the struggle and frustration of those days dealing with the pain, I told myself that something good would come of it, much like Billy Joel and the Piano Man story. Something had to. And without all that pain, I would not have taken that one image. If I didn't have that pain, I would have been walking briskly back to transmit, letting my Sports Illustrated dream slip by. That pain opened the door for success.

That one photograph elevated our business like no other. The reputation boost it gave our company was astounding.

Sometimes our biggest successes are a direct result of our biggest struggles.

Embrace the struggle. They make the best stories. Your story is in your struggle. If you don't have a struggle, you don't have a story.

Who wants to read a book or watch a movie about the guy who had no problems in school, got a great paying job and never struggled?

Success without struggle is boring. Your struggles are simply the awesome chapters in the book about your life.

The Power of a Smile

Our youngest son, Dylan, taught me one of life's great lessons—and he was a two-year-old when he did it. It was the day before his third birthday, and we celebrated with our first one-on-one baseball game together. On a gorgeous, early summer evening, Dylan and I rode the train to PNC Park in downtown Pittsburgh.

As we approached the ticket agent, Dylan smiled and asked the lady if this was her job. He then told her that his dad was taking him to the game for his birthday. "You are just too sweet," the lady responded. She then looked at me and whispered to go ahead to the train. She said it was for his birthday. They waved goodbye to each other with large, happy smiles.

Curious, excited, and filled with life, he immediately turned around to the gentleman seated behind us on the train. He greeted the man with a giant grin, explaining to the second of many people that his birthday was tomorrow. Like a skilled reporter, he asked the man a series of questions. The amused gentleman explained that he was going to the game to work. He ran the scoreboard at the ballpark. The three of us talked for nearly the entire ride about his job. As we said goodbye, the man reached into his pocket and handed Dylan a coupon. It was for a free Pirates hat, a black one that we picked up once we got into the ballpark.

I just laughed as we rode the escalator up toward our seats. But once we stopped by the concession stand to load up on goodies, things started to get strange. As you might have guessed, he engaged the woman preparing our nachos with a smile. As I paid for the food, I saw him tilt his head, scrunch up his little face, and do a wave toward her with his tiny hand. The stressed look on her face disappeared. The lady stopped for a moment, took a breath, and waved back. As I finished paying, he noticed that the giant bag of popcorn had four different flavors in one bag. Amazed by this modern miracle, he grabbed the giant bag to get a closer look. I reached to get it away from him before he accidentally ripped the bag. The woman, noticing his excitement, looked at me with an even bigger smile. She waved me away in a hurry, signaling for him to keep the popcorn. I objected, but she waved even quicker.

"Thank you for your smile, sweetie," she yelled to Dylan.

By now, I was feeling guilty for what was going on. People just keep giving him stuff. And nobody ever gives anything away at those concession stands. Ever. As we jammed our faces with nachos and free popcorn during the first few innings, he just kept smiling. By the fifth inning, it was time to introduce him to The Sweet Spot, our go-to ice-cream place at the ballpark. Fortunately, the counter was too high for him to engage another vendor in conversation. I actually paid for our ice cream and sat down in two random seats to eat the ice cream before it melted. With cheeks covered in the multi-colored birthday cake ice cream, he flipped around to give the older couple behind us a giant grin. They smiled right back and walked right into a buzzsaw.

"How old are you?" the nice lady asked.

"It's my birthday tomorrow! I'm going to be three!" he said.

Fortunately, there wasn't anything they could possibly give him. We were all just enjoying the game. As we cleaned up and headed to our real seats, I felt a tap on my right shoulder.

"For his birthday," the gentleman said. He handed Dylan a $20 bill.

This was all too bizarre. A lady let us onto the train for free. Dylan was given a new hat. A huge bag of popcorn. And now twenty bucks? We actually came home with more money than we had when we started! With his little hands still sticky from an evening of bad food and great times, he fell asleep on my lap during the train ride home.

All night, he didn't ask for anything. He just gave smiles. He made people smile back. He brightened up a struggling person's evening with a smile. Everywhere he went, he brightened someone's day only with a smile.

He didn't ask for anything, but he got everything. All with just a smile.

If you want to do one thing to change your life and other's lives for the better, smile at everyone you meet. Everyone. You just never know what great things will happen for you and them.

10xing Your Income

New worlds open up when your stop trading time for money. As an employee, I didn't own my time. On occasion, I would get calls for freelance or corporate work, but that work occurred while I was already on the clock. I had traded my freedom for the security of the paycheck. It never bothered me before because it paid the bills. But as my connections grew, so did my opportunities for freelance work. Still, I was unable to utilize the connections to our benefit business-wise.

If you remember, my take-home pay from the newspaper was less than $100 per day. Now that we were self-employed, my eyes opened to an entirely different world. Out of the blue, I received a call from a gentleman who owned a local business. I met him a while back on assignment, and he remembered me. A congressman was stopping by his offices later that week to check out operations, stay for lunch, and talk to his employees. Because of our plan to create time freedom, I was available that day for the shoot.

After a brief negotiation, the rate we agreed upon was more than $1,000. Ten times my daily pay at the paper. And this was for one assignment, not my full day.

I showed up for the shoot as I would if I were shooting for the newspaper. I shot in the same style, using the same equipment, capturing the moments the way I did on the job. Not surprisingly, the newspaper sent a photographer, as well. Working side by side with a former co-worker, we traded stories and shared a few laughs during the afternoon. The shoot concluded, and he headed off to his next assignment. I went to dinner with a few friends.

To cover the same exact assignment, in the same exact manner, I was paid ten times what he was paid. He was paid more than nine hundred dollars less than I was— for the same time—and he still needed to photograph another assignment. Plus, I kept the rights to my photographs, which could lead to sales and additional income in the future. He surrendered his rights to the newspaper.

So, what are you giving up in the name of security?

The Golden Day

The Golden Day was an idea that came to me during a pivotal moment in our early years freelancing. We weren't charging enough money, but were working ourselves ragged. Does that sound familiar? It's the freelancer's dilemma. The first issue is getting the work. With grit, determination, some luck, and hustle, most freelancers get the ball rolling. The next issue is what to do once the work is coming in. Is it taking away from your family life or your main job? Is it enough money? Many of us have the desire to turn our freelance business into something big enough that we can leave our job and go into our own business full-time.

So, what do you do when all your time is taken up? Between a job, a side business, and a family, we need a three-ended candle to burn. It's exhausting, overwhelming, and ultimately unsustainable.

It's so easy to give up. When you work as hard as you can and don't see progress, it's easy to lose hope. It's also easy to try to fix everything at once by trying to make big, giant changes.

Let me tell you that nothing good ever comes from losing hope. And although a big splash might feel good, most successes are built from small, consistent, incremental changes. If you are struggling with this situation, your rates are not where they should be, or that you would want them to be. It's almost every freelancer's kryptonite—how do you charge what you're worth? What I want you to decide is what the ideal rate, in a perfect world, would be for your services.

Don't be shy and don't be greedy. The rate you would be thrilled to make. Do you have that number?

That's where the Golden Day comes in.

Now take out your calendar. Take one day this month and mark it as a Golden Day. That day, and that day alone (for now), charge your ideal rate. It would be an extreme bonus if you could leave that day clear and afford not to get hired. Even if it is an existing customer, you can let them know that your schedule is filled, but on this day, the rate is your ideal amount. If you have flexibility, make a few Golden Days that first month. The more you have, the quicker you will elevate your business.

You will learn quickly if you haven't been charging enough. What happened with us, and with nearly everyone we have taught this to, is that your customers won't even bat an eye at the price increase. When that happens, you have now been given the assurance that your rates have been subpar. If one person is willing to pay your ideal rates, who's to say more customers won't?

Here's the caveat—if you work the Golden Day strategy and don't fill those dates, it might be time to look inward. If you are working yourself to the bone, just making ends meet and unable to raise your rates, you need to make some changes in the quality of your services. The level of satisfaction you have provided to your customers is not equal to your desired compensation. It's a reality check that you need to improve in areas that aren't being met.

But if you are reading this, you are not a slacker. I'm confident your issue stems from a lack of confidence as opposed to a lack of quality. So, if you follow the playbook, increase your rates one day a month, fill that date, and gain a bit of confidence, it's time to take your business to the next level. Choose an extra Golden Day the next month and stick to it. As you slowly gain momentum and income, your options expand.

If you do this patiently and methodically, your Golden Days will fill up more of your calendar. This brings you options you weren't afforded before. Your income will rise while working the same amount of days—or fewer. You will be able to go after your business success harder, or choose a few Golden Days to spend with your family.

You have now given yourself options. And one of those options is to create a new Golden Day rate. This is a practice we still employ today. There have been many times we have pushed the limits too far and ended up with a free Golden Day, but once our income was high enough, it was welcomed because we made sure we did a fun family activity that day. It's a win-win situation.

But by starting with just one day a month, it's slow and steady enough to avoid any overwhelming problems. And the results will be extraordinary.

Make People Happy for a Living

Our two intentions when starting our first business were as follows:

1) Make money so we can pay off our debt.
2) Do work where we have more control over our time.

Both of them were logical and moral, and frankly, they worked. But there was an area missing. Ironically, it is the most important one. Subconsciously, I knew about it, but it wasn't something I thought about, or cared to give credence to.

Until a late fall meeting with Penny Sabolsky, the mother of Jaci and Laurie. We had photographed Jaci's wedding a year before, and had just completed Laurie's wedding. Penny is as genuine as they come—loving, thoughtful, generous, and outspoken. One of the things we love most about her is that she tells it like it is.

We met for coffee shortly after the wedding when she handed me an envelope. The wedding was paid in full, so I was confused by the gesture. I thanked her and placed it in my pocket, trying not to be gaudy by opening it in front of her. As she played with Dylan, our five-month-old, she looked at me with a keen interest.

"So how does it feel," Penny asked, "to make people happy for a living?"

I laughed, trying not to take her seriously. She is sarcastically inclined, and I wasn't sure if she was messing with me. But she didn't have a hint of sarcasm in her voice. It wasn't long before we hugged, and she kissed Dylan goodbye. I never did give her an answer. Not once since I started my working life did I think about making people happy. That sounds more selfish than I want it to, but I always thought I should do something that made *me* happy. When I got in my car, I almost forgot the envelope in my pocket until I felt it while sitting down. I pulled out the envelope still thinking about Penny's question.

The check was for more than $1,200.

It was the largest tip we've ever received. I sincerely didn't feel right about her giving us that much money. I called her once I got home, thanking her but letting her know how uncomfortable I felt.

"Don't you see," Penny explained, "it makes *us* feel good to give to *you*. You, of all people, should know how that feels."

I always believed that photography—or any work, for that matter—was something I did for myself. I felt that if people liked it enough, they would hire us. For all these years, I believed that. But Penny taught me, lovingly and generously, that it was how our work made them feel that mattered. That's why they hired us. That's why they loved the work. That's why they were thrilled to part with more than a thousand dollars just to say thank you.

Find a way to make people happy for a living, and you never worry about finding work.

20 Questions

1. Do you practice being better than yesterday?
2. Can you remember a bad assignment that you have given yourself?
3. What lesson(s) did you learn from it?
4. Name an area of your life where you would benefit by doing the opposite?
5. How would an "Hour of Giving" improve your relationships and your business?
6. Who do you need to start saying 'no' to?
7. Do you journal?
8. Do you have an exercise routine in the morning?
9. Do you meditate?
10. What is one thing you can do immediately to make your business better?
11. What is one thing you can do immediately to make your family better?
12. Is there an area of your life that hinders you because you have too many choices?
13. Describe a time in your life where a painful situation turned into a big win.
14. How many books did you read to completion last year?
15. Have you used pain to your advantage?
16. Would those who know you best say you smile enough?
17. Allow yourself to dream for a minute. Is there an area in your business where you can 10x your income while doing the same amount of work?
18. How can you begin to implement that idea?
19. What is your "Golden Day" number?
20. Do you make people happy for a living?

PHASE IV

A LIFE OF FREEDOM

I magine this: you wake up tomorrow morning and all your debts and bills are paid off. You have enough money to live the rest of the year without having to work another day, your investments are fully funded, and you have a large emergency fund. You have money set aside to give.

Your relationships, including the ones with your spouse, children, and friends, are thriving. Not only that, but you have time to devote to them daily and weekly, which will make these relationships better in the future. With this extra time and money, you eat better, exercise more, and get great sleep. As a result, you have gotten into the best shape of your life and are in a better mood. The three areas of life people worry the most about—money, health, and relationships—are the best you've ever experienced.

It's also a day where, if an unexpected emergency comes up, you've created the wiggle room so you can handle it without stress. To top it off, you truly love the work you do. You don't have to work as much, but you do because you love it. Because it fires you up. Because it adds value to others, makes their lives better, and you earn income from it. And because you can be more selective with your time and the clients you work with, you are now earning more than ever while working less.

This is also the point where you really get to make a big life leap. Instead of trading time for money as much, you have the financial and mental freedom to create new business ideas. You have time to devote to personal and business relationships. You have all the advantages that everyone in Phases I, II, and III do not have. It's now all there for the taking. The life you dream of and desire.

This is your life in Phase IV. The benefits are astounding, but there are downfalls if you don't pay attention…

Achieving the Dream

From the beginning of this journey, we had a dream. Everyone needs a dream.

That dream was now a mere ten hours away from reality. The car was packed. Our three boys were bouncing off the couch like it was Christmas Eve. The far-fetched, seemingly impossible goal of being able to shape our business and life—to take big chunks of time off from work to travel with our family—had finally come to fruition. We had finally achieved the financial and time freedom we had long desired and worked for. We were shutting down our business for more than a month and hitting the road!

At 4:00 a.m. the next morning, our family of five left the chilly, wintery Pittsburgh air for the warm beaches of Padre Island in Southeast Texas. For the next month, we would explore the great state of Texas, with our home base being a condo overlooking an inlet of the Gulf of Mexico.

This was the maiden trip of our long-term plan for numerous extended trips to see the world together.

But there was one last thing to do before putting the kids to bed—watch the ultimate Texas movie. You probably guessed it: *Pee Wee's Big Adventure*. If you aren't familiar, the '80s movie is a beyond-goofy comedy about Pee Wee Herman's quest to find his beloved stolen bike. The search takes him to Texas, where he inadvertently becomes a rodeo champion, learns there is no basement in the Alamo, and is at the center of an impromptu sing-a-long of Deep in the Heart of Texas.

But my most memorable line occurs during one of the few serious moments in the flick. Pee Wee and Simone, a waitress he met that evening, are sitting together inside a prehistoric dinosaur exhibit while looking out at the stars. While talking of their aspirations, Simone reveals her biggest dream—to see Paris. Pee Wee asks what was stopping her. She meekly explains that her boyfriend, Andy, is holding her back from going.

"Simone, this is your dream," a suddenly serious Pee Wee pleads. "You have to follow it."

"You're right," Simone agrees, "but…"

"But what?" Pee Wee asks, and then lets out a disappointed sigh. He delivers the line of the movie—and the signature line of our trip—which should be placed at the top of any tough-love manual.

"Everyone I know has a big but."

Our boys howled in laughter. Nolan and Dylan fell off the couch from uncontrollable giggles. Their laughter was so loud that we didn't get to hear the end of the scene. I watched the movie years ago, but I never remembered that line. It had more significance now, after what we had gone through getting to this point. Pee Wee was spot on. When it comes to chasing our dreams, everyone has a big but stopping them.

It wasn't until I watched the clip while writing this story that I finally got to hear what followed his classic comment.

"C'mon, Simone," Pee Wee presses, "let's talk about your big but."

Your Big But

I hope you don't mind me getting personal for a minute, but let's talk about your big but.

Through teaching these lessons and learning them myself, almost every failed plan or venture has a "Yeah, but" attached to it. And the "buts" happen in all different times on this journey.

You can be in Phase I, struggling. Your car is unimpressive to your neighbors. It's unimpressive to you, as well. You have a big decision to make. You got burned with a used car in the past, and you slipped into the dealership to just "look". Suddenly, this big but showed up.

...But We Needed a New Car

"Most people trade their dreams for a car payment."—**Chris Guillebeau**

According to Experian, the average car payment for a new vehicle is $503, and that is for more than five years! Imagine a country where buying a reliable used car with cash replaced this self-inflicted torture brought on by this new-car craze.

I did the math, and it's a pretty sweet country we would be living in. Without the average car payment...

- Five years of saving the $503 car payment would give you a 20% down payment on a $150,000 house.
- If you put that $503 payment into a savings account with no interest from the day your child was born until he or she left for college, you could put more than $100,000 toward their college expenses.
- You could fly your family to Europe once a year.
- If you started putting your car payment into your retirement account starting at age thirty, you would be in the ballpark of $1,000,000 by retirement.
- You could purchase two great seats for the Super Bowl every single year.
- You could give out a $15 gift card to someone every day of the year.
- Every month, you could go to the upper level of your local mall and create havoc by tossing $500 in singles and watch everyone lose their minds.

Can you believe what we give up for something we drive? Something that some dolt who's not paying attention while looking at his phone can mangle or scratch in a nanosecond, or that our kids spill juice all over?

We've driven enough clunkers to know that the need for a new, "reliable" car is a successful sales pitch by car companies. Most cars on the road are reliable, older cars. A new car is, indeed, a want and not a need. I will say, tossing the money from the mall is something we might need to add to our bucket list, now that I think about it.

Or you could be in Phase II, building your business. You could be on track with sales. You could be on your way to freeing up debt and on the road to freedom. You have a baby on the way. And then this big but shows up.

...But We Need a Bigger House

"We're not raising grass. We're raising boys."—Baseball player Harmon Killebrew to his wife after she complained about their boys playing rough in their back yard.

Do we need a bigger house simply because a banker says we can afford the payment? Or because our friends say so? Or because we added another kid to our family? I can tell you with certainty that a new baby doesn't take up very much space. That's a parent thing more than a kid thing. We now culturally justify purchasing an entirely new lifestyle when a little baby comes into our lives. Did your parents buy a new luxury vehicle and a big, beautiful house to have more room to change your diapers and for you to crawl? I didn't think so. Mine didn't either.

A bigger home, as Andy Andrews says, is just a longer walk to the bathroom.

Seriously, though, who wouldn't love a bigger home? I've caught myself daydreaming about it many times. I cruise through these neighborhoods with huge, gorgeous homes, giant lawns, and stunning pools. It might be a coincidence, or just a convenient way for me to look at it, but I never see anyone playing in those big giant yards or swimming in those awesome pools. I can't help but wonder if it's because they have to spend so much time working that they can't enjoy it enough.

Having the biggest, the best, and the nicest doesn't always make sense, either, especially while raising children. We don't have a fancy house, and aren't interested in a fancy house right now. We're raising three boys. My egotistical reasons for wanting a bigger house are only for status. I see these houses and grow envious, but we got here by not keeping up with the Joneses. Why start now?

Maybe you've noticed it, but the Joneses are broke. They are stressed out. They are in debt up to their eyeballs. They don't spend time together. They have nice cars but no freedom. They might have a bigger house, but I want you to have less stress, more time, and more money to do the things you love.

We do dream, and some of those dreams are about the next house. We have a vision of what our next step will be. We talk about it, work for it, and plan for it, but when we get there, the idea is to pay for it with our money, not money we borrow. No possession—not even the dream house—is worth being a money slave ever again.

And if you are trying to impress people with the way your house looks, I'd recommend you shift and try to impress them by the way your house sounds.

The Wise Man Next Door

Dr. Thomas Stanley was a researcher, university professor, and author of seven books, among them the brilliant study of millionaires in America titled *The Millionaire Next Door*, which he co-wrote with William Danko. The book was an eye-opening study of the habits of those who have accumulated great wealth.

The book changed my perception of who the rich really are in this country. What we hear most often about the wealthy are the houses and the cars and the bling. But that's not reality.

Stanley and Danko revealed that the vast, overwhelming majority of millionaires got that way by modesty, frugality, and prudence.

The millionaires of this nation—the majority of millionaires—lived on less than they made.

They lived in homes in middle-class neighborhoods where most of their neighbors didn't have a clue they were that wealthy. But what about all those huge, glamorous houses we admire from afar? For many, they would be what the book termed "Big Hat, No Cattle."

That's an expression Stanley picked up from a wealthy business owner in Texas describing the people who act rich. This business owner dressed no differently than his employees and was often mistaken as one. Big hat, no cattle might be translated as "Big house, no money" outside Texas.

Stanley and Danko unearthed some mind-blowing information about who the wealthy in this nation really are.

Check this out. Most millionaires drive a two-year-old, or older, automobile. Almost two-thirds of millionaires are self-employed, even though only twenty percent of the population is self-employed. That alone is one of the best correlations between self-employment and financial success. The businesses these people own are not glamorous. Contractors, farmers, auctioneers. Not what we might have expected.

The average millionaire in this country is a 57-year-old male, married, with three children, and has a net worth of $3.7 million with an average taxable income of $131,000 per year.

They also live on less than seven percent of their wealth. Almost all of them (97%) are homeowners, with a home valued at an average of $320,000. Do these sound like the millionaires who are publicized?

Most millionaires (88%) are first-generation rich and never received an inheritance. A small minority lease cars, and the majority believe that getting out of debt is the greatest advantage to building wealth. Four out of five are college graduates, but only 17% ever attended a private elementary school or high school. Almost two-thirds still work 45-55 hours per week and invest 20% of their income each year.

One of the most glaring observations was that they defined being wealthy differently than the majority of Americans. The millionaires did not define being wealthy in terms of material possessions. It was determined that more people who have lifestyles based around consumption have little to no investments, assets, or private businesses. The people who are wealthy own tremendous amounts of appreciative assets and shun a high-consumption lifestyle.

When it comes to family, it's not like television either. In the typical millionaire household, the wives are meticulous budgeters and are more conservative with the money than the husband.

They also refuse to subsidize irresponsible children. They are more likely to financially assist their daughters because men make more within the same occupational categories. They believe men don't need the support because the financial world favors them.

I would imagine the real millionaires in the United States would be considered incredibly dull compared to the outrageous, high-flying personalities placed in front of us throughout the internet and television. It makes sense, I suppose, because ratings and ad revenue are what seem to matter. That's all cool. It's their business. The real issue is that, after a while, the viewers actually believe the perception. Except it's not the reality.

Thomas Stanley's thorough research uncovered the true millionaires in America and went on to sell more than three million copies, helping families like ours avoid the consumption trap that has snared a large portion of our society. His research still hasn't received the attention it deserves.

If you have a moment, take a second to appreciate what this gentleman gave to all of us. He helped us undress the notion that you have to be an unethical, cigar-toting, ruthless businessman, a famous athlete, or a talented musician to make it in this country.

You Already Have Everything You Need

Somewhere, someone is happier than you are with less than you have. Be happy now. It's good for your health, and it's attractive.

My friend, David McLain, who is a globe-traveling National Geographic photographer, told me a story years ago that has never left my brain. He told me about his time backpacking across India, living comfortably on a few dollars a day. He had traveled all over the world and noticed the demeanor of the people living there.

"They were the happiest people I have ever met," he told me during dinner one evening. "Much happier than people here."

I didn't believe him. I couldn't understand how people living in what we would consider abject poverty could even be remotely happy. He explained that they had everything they needed. To us they seem poor, but they do not feel poor.

Happiness to them does not come from things they can purchase. They don't even know what they're doing without, so they don't compare. Comparison truly is the thief of joy. They simply choose to be happy.

So, can you choose to be happy? The place to start, and remain, is to be happy but not satisfied.

Be happy where you are while working for what you desire. It will get you there much quicker than complaining. And if you can't find a way to enjoy what you do now, you will most likely struggle even when you achieve your greatest dreams and desires.

Most importantly, happier people live longer and better lives. Harvard psychologist Laura Kubzansky, who studies optimism, discovered some amazing results. She found that optimists have half the rate of heart disease as pessimists, which had the same difference as smokers to non-smokers. Optimists also have stronger immune systems, lower blood pressure, catch fewer infectious diseases, and live on average ten years longer than pessimists.

I guess Bobby McFerrin had it right all along. Don't worry. Be happy.

Pat Flynn, the author of *Will It Fly* and the host of the uber-successful podcasts *Smart Passive Income* and *Ask Pat*, is someone who gets it. Flynn posts his income report each month on the top right hand corner of his SPI website. As I write this, the income number looking back at me is 157,131.95. For the month. Not too shabby, eh?

This isn't a recent outlier success. Flynn has been posting these numbers for years, and they have always been impressive. Pat's income clearly eclipses the vast majority of the population.

In a recent episode of SPI, Pat was asked to describe what his best day ever would look like.

With his income, the possibilities are endless. Everything is on the table.

But his answer might surprise you.

"My best day ever," Pat responded, quickly and confidently "would be with my family, on a lake, fishing somewhere where I have never fished. Just peaceful on a lake with my entire family, Dad and Mom included. We're eating sandwiches, and I'm drinking a beer. That would be a perfect day."

Maybe it took making six figures a month to figure it out, or maybe Flynn has always been grounded and down to earth. But the sooner we learn to be happy with the simple things in life, the better life will be.

The Mexican Fisherman

On the first three-generational road trip of my fatherhood, my dad, two-year-old son Andrew, and I took a drive to Bowling Green, Kentucky to visit the Corvette Museum. We stopped into Jimmy John's to grab a few sandwiches before checking out the fleet of classic automobiles. As my dad graciously took care of the bill, I held Andrew in my arms as I spied a story, printed and framed, on the wall. It forever changed my outlook on how I thought about the business world.

An American investment banker was at the pier of a small coastal Mexican village when a small boat with just one fisherman docked. Inside the small boat were several large yellowfin tuna. The American complimented the Mexican on the quality of his fish and asked how long it took to catch them. The Mexican replied, "Only a little while."

The American then asked why didn't he stay out longer and catch more fish. The Mexican said he had enough to support his family's needs. The American asked, "But what do you do with the rest of your time?"

The Mexican fisherman said, "I sleep late, fish a little, play with my children, take siestas with my wife, stroll into the village each evening where I sip wine and play guitar with my amigos. I have a full and busy life."

The American scoffed. "I am a Harvard MBA and could help you. You should spend more time fishing, and with the proceeds, buy a bigger boat. With the proceeds from the bigger boat, you could buy several boats. Eventually, you would have a fleet of fishing boats."

"Instead of selling your catch to a middleman, you would sell directly to the processor, eventually opening your own cannery. You would control the product, processing, and distribution. You would need to leave this small coastal fishing village and move to Mexico City, then L.A., and eventually New York City, where you will run your expanding enterprise."

The Mexican fisherman asked, "But, how long will this all take?"

To which the American replied, "Fifteen to twenty years."

"But what then?" asked the Mexican.

The American laughed and said, "That's the best part. When the time is right, you would announce an IPO and sell your company stock to the public and become very rich. You would make millions!"

"Millions. Then what?"

The American said, "Then you would retire. Move to a small coastal fishing village where you would sleep late, fish a little, play with your kids, take siestas with your wife, and stroll to the village in the evenings where you could sip wine and play guitar with your amigos."

The Responsibility of Freedom

"Discipline is freedom."—Jocko Willink

With freedom comes great responsibility. When you reach Phase IV, you now have the option to become complacent, and it wouldn't really hurt anything. You have the ability to do nothing for long periods of time, and you might take advantage of that!

And after all those years being a time slave, who would blame you? For me, that time lasted for two years. I loved the freedom! But there came a sense of dissatisfaction. I convinced myself to work as little as possible. We made it to the point that I didn't need to work outside the home more than fifteen days a year.

But after a while, it was an empty feeling. I knew I didn't want to do more of the same assignments, but I needed to do something. This was where I finally got to determine my ideal day, every day. To answer that question, "If money didn't matter and you could do anything you want every day, what would you do?"

I finally had the ability to figure myself out. That was something I had never thought about, and maybe you haven't either. You just needed to go to work and pay the bills. Who has time to think about what your life is about? But now, with your newfound freedom, you have the time.

But if you are anything like me, this can come with a dark side. When you finally have time to discover who you are, you don't always like what you see. Besides Phase I, this has the potential to be the most difficult phase. But it is also the most rewarding. With nothing holding you back, you finally get the chance to see what your full potential is, and that can be scary. It's difficult to abuse scarcity, but it's easy to abuse abundance.

This is where you get to take yourself to a higher level. You get to determine your purpose in life beyond just working a job and making money to survive. It's also the stage where building wealth becomes easy.

Must Be Nice

When you reach Phase IV, you will begin to have some haters. Believe it or not, not everyone will be excited for your success. It's something you will have to deal with as you exit the rat race toward your life of freedom.

There was always one phrase that got under my skin.

"Must be nice."

If you ever find yourself wanting to say that, stop yourself. As much as you will hurt the person you say it to, it will hurt you more. Successful people don't envy other's successes, they celebrate them. Trust me, I've said that phrase often enough in the past. When things weren't going in the direction I wanted, it was so easy to look at someone doing better and say, "Must be nice."

When I jealously uttered that passive-aggressive phrase, it only meant that I wanted what they had—I was just too lazy to work for it.

The Beautiful Day Rule

We have very few rules in our business, but one is of huge importance. We named it "The Beautiful Day Rule".

It's a simple rule. If there is a beautiful day outside, we have the freedom to enjoy it. If we have imminent work that needs to be completed, it gets top priority so we can enjoy the day. Otherwise, we are to be free on beautiful days. It doesn't mean we can't work, or that we won't work—it just means that we have a hall pass to get outside and enjoy a beautiful day. When you were trapped in school on a gorgeous day, is there anything you valued more than a pass to get out and enjoy the sunshine? Me neither.

The wonderful thing about The Beautiful Day Rule is that it made us more efficient in our business. If we lived in San Diego, that might be different because every day is gorgeous outside. But we never lived in San Diego, so we didn't have that problem. Being that we live in Pittsburgh, we know that the potential for a beautiful day is always on the horizon, so we budget our time to knock out as much as we can early in the morning, or on rainy days. If the weatherman says that tomorrow is going to be a great day to go outside, we sometimes do our work in the evening just to free up the next day. Imminent work is handled promptly and knocked out, and with the advantage of both of us in the business, there is no doubt that at least one of us will get the hall pass.

So, when we finally have a chance to thumb our noses at the system, we do it. Not having a boss to agitate anymore with requests for repeated days off, I still need someone to instigate, even if it is an invisible 'system'. And what good is freedom if you can't enjoy it?

The Beautiful Day Rule has given us more awesome memories than I can count. If we kept the employee mindset, we would have continued staring at a computer screen as those days passed us by.

A wonderful part about making your own business means you can make your own rules—and if you are going to make a rule, you might as well make it a fun one.

Creating Uncommon Options

"Work doesn't have a memory, but your family does."—**Aaron Walker**

The thing about the ideal life dream is that it changes. When I was single, the ideal life was one of constant traveling, late nights out and, well, I can't remember much more than that. Having a wife and three boys, the ideal life became dramatically different. In my twenties, I might have looked at the life I'm living today as totally boring when, in fact, it's the most exciting time of my life. I now look back on the lifestyle of my twenties and cringe about how shallow it seemed, but I had a blast with no regrets. My life today would never have turned out this way without the lessons, successes, and struggles of those past days.

Crafting your ideal life requires a vision of the future. If you are growing, your life today will not be the same life you will desire five, ten, fifteen years from now.

Elizabeth and I crafted a plan once we began our family, and even though the core values like time and money freedom and a life based on experiences have not changed, so many other variables have come into play. And not being beholden to money or an employer has allowed us to pursue those dreams and continue to achieve them.

When our oldest boys were very little, our main goal was to remain self-employed through their time in first grade. The way we viewed it then was, if we can raise them at home without daycare until we get them on that bus for a full day of school, we won. Just don't screw up the business. If either of us needed to get a job again, we couldn't sustain the business, and everything would be thrown for a loop. So, the short-term goal was very simple: don't screw up the business. But we weren't able to see that what we wanted now might be totally different than what we might want a few years from now.

Fast forward a few years. We succeeded with our goal. Our two oldest boys were on the bus for school, and our little guy, Dylan, was now three. Once Dylan got on that bus, we thought we were free, right? Elizabeth and I sipped coffee and thought about what we would do again with so much free time. We thought about expanding the business, going out to lunch, and meeting with friends during the day. I'd play a bunch of guitar. It was the perfect plan. We noticed something, though, that made us a little uncomfortable. When the kids got off the bus, everything was so rushed. Homework was immediately followed by dinner. And heaven forbid there was some type of extracurricular activity going on after school. By January, Elizabeth and I realized something after the kids went to bed. We hardly got to see them anymore.

Now, in this day and age, that sounds pretty normal, but we never set out to be normal. It was around that time I met Ken Carfagno, who is now one of my closest friends. He was working crazy hours on his cleaning business while writing early in the morning on the book he would soon publish, an interactive book for parents and children titled Arctic Land.

Ken and his wife, Teresa, have five kids, and they homeschool. His oldest son, Kenny, kept his schoolbooks next to his bed and began his work as soon as he got up. Ken told me about the time Teresa gets with them, how closely they have bonded, and how they have accelerated with their studies. He warned me not to have my wife talk to his wife because she is the "homeschool whisperer." If you talk with Teresa, he said, you will be called to homeschool your kids.

It all sounded too crazy. We had never given one thought to homeschooling. Isn't that what school, and our school taxes, are for? We've heard all the negative stereotypes, but I don't think we've known anyone who actually did it. Until now. This was certainly not in our plan, but it sounded incredibly interesting. Elizabeth and I realized one of our big, giant goals as a family was to travel often with our kids. Our eyebrows raised at the thought of long November and February vacations instead of going in the summer with everyone else. We thought of the one-on-one days that would happen once the work from the day is done. The positives began to severely outweigh the negatives. The big struggle was going to be the loss of the free time that we had been so desperately looking forward to.

With me taking on much of the work Elizabeth did in the business, that time we had worked for might be lost.

This was where having options truly came into play. When homeschooling became a true option in our heads, we sat down while they were at school and asked ourselves a series of questions.

Why are we doing all of this? Are we doing it just to make more money? Our business already gives us what we need. Do we need more money while having less time with the kids? Are we fine with twelve-fifteen more years of time-crunched evenings and rushed mornings getting the kids on the bus, so we get all that time for ourselves? We knew we were fortunate even to consider that decision. If we had been in a bunch of debt and working at jobs outside the home, this wouldn't be possible.

But freedom made it possible. And now we had a choice to make.

It didn't take long. We decided we would start homeschooling the following year.

This was not part of the original plan, but the ability to choose and change has now given us the ultimate in lifestyle freedom. We aren't beholden to a work schedule or the kids' school schedule. Now, if we want to take a trip to Chicago, or just spend the day in the stream catching crayfish at Mingo Creek State Park, we have that choice.

The kids are working harder than ever on subjects they love doing. It's more than we could have expected. And many days they drive us nuts. Elizabeth and I don't get all the quiet time we were looking for, but there's plenty of time for that. For us, this was what mattered. With every choice, we are choosing to do something, and at the same time, choosing not to do everything else.

Dreams Change

Dreams and goals change. There was a time when I couldn't imagine being anything career-wise but a professional photographer. And if we would have stayed financially stressed, I wouldn't have had other options. If my job or business went away, I would have been scrounging for the next assignment, likely at lower pay.

But freedom brings options. My career as a photographer was better than ever, but it took up much less time than before. Ironically, we made more money than in the past while working much less. I only accepted the assignments I wanted, so that opened up time, as well. Each year, we accept less weddings and corporate assignments than the year before.

That time, though, was not spent shooting or studying photography. I spend that time on the phone, in person, or online helping others grow their businesses and create more time in their busy lives. I could be on the phone for hours, and completely lose track of time.

On June 9th, 2016, I was credentialed to photograph the first potential championship-clinching game in Pittsburgh in more than fifty years. The

Pittsburgh Penguins were one win away, and the Stanley Cup was down the hallway from my pre-game set-up area. This was the assignment I always wanted, and here it finally was.

But as exciting as that day was, I was just as jacked up about the two phone calls from the day before where I got to help people with their business and personal breakthroughs. That was hard to comprehend.

And as the intensity of that night carried on, I couldn't believe the level of gratitude I had for this life I'd been given. There was a time when an assignment like that would have come with a huge adrenaline buildup, and the eventual letdown as I faded back into the mundane. The Penguins lost that game, by the way, so, there was no celebration.

But the diversity that following this Freelance to Freedom plan has given to us was astounding. The day before, I was fulfilled by coaching. The days after, I wrote some of the words you are reading in this book. A night later, our family was in the back yard roasting s'mores, catching fireflies, and listening to the Penguins win the cup in San Jose on the radio. Days later, I was assigned to photographed the Stanley Cup victory parade.

But I realized the night of the game that photography didn't define me or my career any longer. These steps to freedom afforded me the opportunity to dig into the different areas of my life that I had longed to explore—writing, coaching, and building meaningful relationships, in addition to photography. Freedom gives me the flexibility to choose daily what I want to work on, achieve, and accomplish. It gives me the opportunity to create income in various ways, so that I'm not beholden to one industry or career. It allows my wife and I to lay our heads on our pillows each night and decide what it is we want to do the next day, and each day afterward.

20 Questions

1. Are you living your dream?
2. What is a goal that used to seem so unattainable, but is now possible?
3. Are you 100% debt free?
4. Do you have everything you need?
5. Do you have a big but in your life?
6. Has your newfound freedom allowed you to figure yourself out better?
7. Do you notice less stress in your life since attaining freedom?
8. Do you see what your full potential is?
9. Are you able to help more people, either with time or money, better than you used to?
10. Has anyone said "Must be nice" to you lately?
11. Have you said "Must be nice" to someone lately?
12. Do you believe that you already have everything you need?
13. What is something you used to do that you no longer enjoy and are financially able to let go of because of your freedom?
14. What uncommon options has freedom created for you?
15. What responsibilities has freedom brought to your life?
16. Do you have a "Beautiful Day Rule", or something similar?
17. Are you more like the millionaire next door, or the millionaire Thomas Stanley refers to as "Big Hat, No Cattle?"
18. What drives you besides money and success?
19. What uncommon options has this freedom created in your life?
20. What would getting to Phase V look like for you?

PHASE V

EVERY DAY IS INDEPENDENCE DAY

In Phase I, you struggled in a job or career you didn't want. Money was tight and time was a struggle. In Phase II, you started your side business and got the ball rolling. In Phase III, your business grew and you left your job. You paid off debt. You started optimizing your business, creating more time freedom and building wealth. In Phase IV, you created time freedom, as well as money freedom. You have no debt and are in complete control of your schedule. Even in Phase IV, you are trading your time for money. You are doing it to a lesser degree than in the earlier phases, but you are still location-dependent. In Phase V, it all comes together.

You thought Phase IV sounded good with no debt, time freedom, wealth-building, and control over your time every day? Well, what if you were able to add location freedom to your life?

What You Think Is Ordinary...

"What you think is ordinary is amazing to others."—Derek Sivers

By becoming an expert in your field, you have not only created the business and life you desire, you created a blueprint for many others to do what you have done. In Phases I-IV, you were unknowingly writing the course that will positively impact the lives of potentially millions of people.

And now you get to teach that. From anywhere. With less stress, less need for income (which is always when the highest income arrives), and the ability to shape your exact vision. You don't have to mess with venture capitalists to prop up what you do. You don't need to adjust your plans because you lack time or money.

Think about that. You have built the ultimate foundation. You have no debt. You have complete control over your time. You have money in the bank, and your investments are rocking. You are an expert in your field, and being an expert in any subject has major perks. You've already taken gobs of time off, and realized that laying on the beach every day, being unproductive, eventually gets old.

You get to choose what you do every day. And you have this thing called the internet.

The possibilities are endless. Teaching, coaching, speaking, writing, online courses, accepting only the jobs you love or the ones that pay the best. It's all there. All things that help others, generate income, and allow you to do work you love. And you get to set yourself apart from the majority of the people doing these things because you aren't desperate for money, and you actually are the expert teaching the material.

This was how we transitioned into Phase V. I spoke early in the book about building the foundation. When you build it strong and you have plans, goals, and a strategy, your skyscraper will one day be a towering success. When it's highly visible, people take notice.

Our coaching business happened organically, built from previous successes. Like before, we built a product that sold itself. When you figure out what others want to learn, you become an authority. People seek you out for knowledge. People ask you to develop products for them to purchase. People pay you money to learn from you about what you have already done.

And with no debt, money in the bank, a flexible schedule, and time freedom, the options are limitless. The idea of taking a month-long vacation with our family, and creating the same income—if not more—was once a dream. The Freelance to Freedom plan made it a reality.

What Day Is It?

Looking back, it was only a month after our journey out of debt ended and our life of freedom began that Elizabeth and I realized how truly special having that freedom was. We packed lunches, towels, sunscreen, toys, and two little boys to head to the park for an impromptu afternoon picnic.

Elizabeth took pictures of Nolan crawling through the beautiful purple flowers covering the landscape at the park. Andrew and I tossed bread off the dock to the fish below, laughing together as their giant mouths opened in anticipation. I looked around and noticed a jogger and a few grandparents walking with their grandkids. Otherwise, the park was all ours for this perfect afternoon.

"Dad," Andrew asked while holding my hand as we walked off the dock, "what day is today?"

"Andrew," I responded with embarrassment, "I don't know!"

When we got back to Elizabeth and Nolan, I asked her the same question. I was curious to see if she knew what day it actually was.

She didn't know either.

It was at that point that what we had done hit me. For the first time since I stepped onto a school bus, someone else wasn't telling me where to go every day. Sure, there was work to do, things to accomplish, and dreams to chase, but we were in charge of when that work would happen.

That evening, I learned that it was Thursday. Eight years later, we practice daily to never lose sight of the blessings that following this plan has afforded us as a family.

Are You Going to Work?

It was a sun-drenched, perfectly crafted California morning. After photographing the Anaheim Ducks hockey game the night before, I was making my way to Phoenix to shoot the Arizona Diamondbacks game the next evening. As the sun briefly crept behind the only clouds in the sky, I pulled into the drive-thru at a local coffee shop. The cheerful barista greeted me with unexpected energy as she prepared a vanilla latte for my drive.

Are you headed to work this morning?" she asked with a smile.

And I found myself not knowing how to answer her. Technically, no, I wasn't going to work. I was on a five-game, six-day trip through Southern California and Arizona to photograph baseball and hockey games for my book *One Shot*. I wasn't being paid for any of the games, so the expenses were on me.

Through the years of relationships and connections, I had been credentialed for each game through different avenues. That is the power of building a network before you need it.

One Shot began during my years as a newspaper photojournalist. It has taken me all over the nation, photographing games at more than 140 professional stadiums. I've been on the field photographing the Super Bowl, the World Series, the Kentucky Derby, the NBA playoffs, The Final Four, and the Stanley Cup Final. It's given me ringside access to WrestleMania, locker rooms for championship celebrations, and behind-the-scenes moments with some of the most famous athletes in the world.

So, I thought about her question again. I explained that I was going to photograph a baseball game.

"That's got to be so cool to do what you love for a living!" she responded.

I headed west toward Arizona, thinking mostly about that conversation. My book, which won't be completed for a few years, might indeed bring in money, but I wasn't getting paid for the work I was doing while I was doing it. It's a difficult concept to explain. This is a project I want for myself more than I want for income.

The lifestyle I'm living thanks to the five phases of *Freelance to Freedom* is hard for me to understand sometimes. I mean, really, how many people have the time to fly out to the West Coast for a week, do exactly what they love for a work project, and pay for it yourself without needing income from the project?

Was I working on that trip? I guess that's up to someone else to decide.

Be Water

"You must be shapeless, formless, like water. When you pour water in a cup, it becomes the cup. When you pour water in a bottle, it becomes the bottle. When you pour water in a teapot, it becomes the teapot. Water can drip, and it can crash. Become like water, my friend."—**Bruce Lee**

Freedom allows you to be water. Freedom allows you to be shapeless, formless, like Lee describes. It allows you to become whatever you want to become. If you want to write, it allows you to write. If you want to travel, it allows you to travel. If you want to raise your kids in your ideal manner, it allows you to raise your kids in your ideal manner.

Freedom means you no longer have to fit into a cup when you want to be in the bottle. It means you no longer have to drip when you want to crash. Freedom means you get to be exactly what you want to be.

Remember, humans have one unifying idea: we all want to control our own destiny. Be water, my friend.

Choose freedom.

Moving Forward

Is it possible for anyone to go from a low-paying job, deeply in debt, stressed out, and hopeless to having a life of financial, time, and location freedom? The cynics will declare that everyone won't do this. And they are probably right. Everyone won't do this.

But anyone can.

The freelance world has never been a more exciting place. The options are virtually unlimited. If you are part of the 80% of Americans unhappy with their job, there is a way out. If you are one of those who longs to run your own show, it can be done better now than ever before. But to succeed, it's essential to control your money and vital that you control your time. And it's absolutely necessary to have your health and relationships thriving.

If you are in debt, crunched for time, and stressed out, standard employment offers limited options. Your employer still control your time. They still decide your income ceiling. They still own your ideas. They can pull the rug out from under your life as fast as you can yell pink slip, and even a pay raise is just tightening the golden handcuffs if you have bigger dreams beyond their company.

To the traditionalist, self-employment is scary and unpredictable. To the self-employed, it's the only way. My friend, Michael O'Neal, the host of the popular *The Solopreneur Hour* podcast, says it well.

"I've seen too much to ever go back. I would be fired immediately from any job now. Because once I gained control of my time, money, and decisions, I became entirely unemployable."

I want you to join us in the ranks of the free and the unemployable.

One of the first steps to freedom is being in control of your money. Can you believe that we went to school for twelve to twenty years but were never taught how to be financially successful? Instead, we were trained to get a job and follow along. Shouldn't handling, investing, and giving money have been important topics to toss into the curriculum? How did we miss that as a culture? If you have control of your money, you have control of your life.

I wrote this to share with you the struggles and successes of what it's like to go through the fire and come out on the other side strong and thriving. Money is only one part of this, but financial stress is the number one reason for divorce in the United States. Stress leads to failed health and failed relationships. Why is self-employment so vital to this process? *Remember that almost two-thirds of millionaires are self-employed, even though only twenty percent of the population is self-employed.*

Now, being a millionaire isn't a guarantee for having no stress. It comes with its own set of unique challenges. But being financially secure gives you more options, more time, and less stress—if you are prepared. And that's what I want for your life. Give it a shot. If you become a millionaire and don't like it, you can always give it all away.

But these steps are useless without changing bad habits. Nobody intentionally sets out to have six figures of debt. Nobody longs for a strained relationship with their spouse. Nobody plans to drive to a job every morning that they hate. No father plans to spend only seven minutes a day with their children while spending more than five hours a day staring at their television or phone.

Nobody ever creates a plan to be normal. You only become normal by not having a plan. And normal is debt. Normal is stress. Normal is overweight. Normal is sick. Normal is dissatisfaction.

Normal is hopeless.

Please do me one favor: don't be normal. It's easy to be normal. Nobody will give you a hard time for being normal. Being normal doesn't make those around you uncomfortable. It's easy to fit in.

But it's impossible to stand out.

****

There are so many thoughts, ideas, and lessons that I want you to take from this book, but I want to end with a story that happened after I finished the first draft. This story takes me back to that pivotal comment my father made to me when I was at a career crossroads right before Andrew was born.

"You have a skill, but you aren't using that skill correctly."

And I feel that is the same for most people who are struggling. We all are standing on our own acre of diamonds.

From the beginning of this book, and weaved throughout, are stories of my career as a sports photographer. It's never been a lucrative part. In all honesty, the pay has always been poor compared to every other area of our business.

But I've always loved it. The stories and experiences I've gained through these assignments are more valuable and precious than anything I could have gained making six figures in some sterile office. I've been assigned to photograph and hang around icons like Muhammad Ali, LeBron James, Wayne Gretzky, Michael Jordan, and Tom Brady, to name just a few. I've been assigned to shoot Super Bowls, the World Series, and every major sporting event across the United States.

And as terrible as the pay was—and still is—it's a passionate part of my career. A part I never wanted to let go of, even when it seemed like nothing but a low-paying ego trip. Somehow, I knew it had value. I knew, in some way, it was an acre of diamonds.

And then I heard my dad's voice again. I had a skill, but I wasn't using that skill correctly.

I noticed that many of my friends were tremendously excited by the photographs and stories I was compiling. Elizabeth and I would go to parties, and I was introduced as the guy who worked on the sidelines and traveled to photograph these famous athletes. Strangers were always asking questions about how they can shoot pictures like I did. People would ask to hear the same stories I'd told over and over, and they never seemed to get old. Except for Elizabeth. They certainly got old to her. Sorry, honey.

Aaron Walker, who was my mastermind group leader, questioned why I didn't teach what I knew. He seemed astounded by it all. He assured me that people would clamor for it if I put it out. A few years earlier, I wrote an outline for an online course for sports photography, but not having any clue how to do it, it sat lonely inside of an Evernote document. So, I shrugged off Aaron's advice, just like that farmer walking past those interesting rocks on his farm before looking for diamonds somewhere else.

A few months after I finished the first draft of *Freelance to Freedom*, I attended a retreat for my mastermind group. In rural Tennessee, Aaron introduced me to Kyle Shultz. Kyle owns Shultz Photo School, a highly successful online photo school. Kyle and I talked during dinner. He listened to my presentation about my career, and then he explained his life and business to the group the following day.

After he spoke, the idea that had bounced around my mind for two years started bouncing around again. I turned toward Kyle and said four words.

"I have an idea…"

"Yes," he responded confidently.

"You don't even know what I'm going to say," I said with a smile.

"Alright. Go ahead," he replied, smiling back. It's like he knew what I was going to say.

"Why don't we do a sports photography course together for your school?"

"Yes," he answered in that same calm manner. "That's exactly what I was thinking."

Within a thirty-second conversation, a new opportunity arose. Twenty-three years in the making, but seemingly created in less than a minute.

I had thought about doing the sports photography course for years, but I didn't have a clue how to create one, build a following, and make it a success. Kyle, it turned out, had planned on offering a sports course at his school for the past two years. He had done and mastered all the things I was clueless about, while I had a full career as a sports photographer to build the course around.

What stopped me earlier? I believed that I needed to do everything myself. I still thought like a freelancer, not an entrepreneur. I believed that the only way to make income from sports photography was through the assignments that I photographed. It didn't cross my mind that there are thousands of beginners who want to take better sports photographs. Or all the parents who are frustrated trying to take better photographs of their kids playing sports. Many of these people are more than willing—even excited—to buy that guidance from someone who photographs the pros for a living.

Kyle recognized what I could bring to his business. He saw something that I took for granted. What we think is ordinary, others think is extraordinary. Similarly, I was immediately in awe and impressed by what he had done. He is brilliant at creating a thriving online community, building funnels, and creating killer courses. He's incredibly humble, but what he had built was nothing short of remarkable. What he saw as ordinary in himself, I saw as extraordinary. What I saw as ordinary in myself, he saw as extraordinary.

Yesterday, while I put the last touches on the final manuscript for *Freelance to Freedom*, the sports photography course launched. And in one day, the course brought in more money than my entire yearly salary as a newspaper photographer.

All of my knowledge, experience and passion towards my craft was worth $32,000 a year in the corporate world. But a course offered to the public with the same knowledge brought in more than $32,000 in less than twenty four hours.

And as exciting as that is, the most exciting part is that I truly believe that we all are standing on our own acres of diamonds. Everyone has developed a talent. Everyone. But most of us either don't recognize it, or aren't using it correctly. What my dad saw in me I can now see everywhere.

So, I ask you the question my father asked me: what skill have you developed that you aren't using correctly?

I see accomplished teachers, musicians and artists struggling with low-paying jobs while there is a need for specific, well-paid tutors, whether in person or online. Work that could be created around their schedule that would benefit their clients and their family. I see people quietly battling addiction alone, while growing and learning, as an entire culture is in desperate need for leaders. I see talented artists pushing their dreams—and other's needs—aside to stare at a screen doing work they despise for eight hours to pay for a lifestyle of consumption while their art and skills remains hidden. I could go on and on.

Everyone has a skill, and on the other side of every skill is a group of people searching for someone to help them. Most of us have so much potential and promise that we take what is special about us for granted while living lives of quiet desperation.

It's time for that to stop. Hopefully for you, that ends when you close this book.

WIN

I've written in detail about the five phases of *Freelance to Freedom* in Part II, but I want to end by giving you a quick, seven-step guide as a fast reference for when you need a quick jolt of inspiration during a tough time, or just to stay on course.

1. Unearth your acre of diamonds.

What is a skill you developed that you don't recognize? Or that you downplay? What is a skill others see, but you take for granted? What is the thing you would do for free, but others would pay for? Find that, and you have found your acres of diamonds.

2. Use your developed talents to help someone who needs it.

Most people fail at this level because they are thinking about what they want and need. They are stressed for time and money, so they think in the short-term. Short-term thinking never leads to great long-term results. That's why payday loans, the lottery, and casinos are so profitable. If you want to succeed, think long-term. And think about what others want. Just remember that nobody will pay you for anything because it's your passion. They will pay when your passion is used to help them solve their needs, wants, and struggles.

3. Take that need and create the career you desire.

Figuring this out can be so simple that we don't even see it. Look around. What do people need?

What is it that you are capable of that can solve this need? What have you been developing, even without realizing it, that can help someone two steps behind where you are? A common pushback is that it's not a "passion", but passion is a dangerous word. Passion can be a selfish word. If your passion comes from solving others' problems, you have won the battle that most artists lose.

4. Use that income from your career to wipe out your debt and become financially free.

The truth is that hardly anyone does this. We say we want to, but we don't. It's so ingrained in the consumer culture that the idea of paying off all our debt has been deemed impossible, even impractical. There are actually people who advise you not to pay off debt. Let that sink in for a moment. They say it's a positive thing to owe money to someone else. Never mind that the people advising us to do so stand to lose income if you do. I won't name the professionals that suggest this, but you can probably figure that out.

If you follow my advice, your debt is gone as soon as humanly possible. All of it, house included. The point is to have a lifetime of freedom, not extreme wealth at seventy-five while regretting the past fifty years of work and lost time to get it. Would you trade a few years of pain for a lifetime of freedom?

5. Use that financial freedom to create time freedom.

This is where it gets fun. When money isn't stressful, creativity flows. It's hard to be creative when you are financially stressed. When money isn't a worry, opportunities appear. It's like the universe finally trusts you with money and starts opening doors for you. You have more money to spend on self-improvement. You have more time to build relationships. With those relationships, and your lack of desperation, you build trust. You get to move at a steady, determined pace. Being patient and persistent, joining masterminds with driven achievers, and thinking of ideas makes opportunities show up. Just like my collaboration with Kyle, they become bigger and more lucrative because you have more time and financial freedom. Remember: Success attracts. Desperation repels.

6. Use your time freedom to help build a stronger family and deeper relationships.

Most people cite money problems as their biggest stress, but in my years digging deep into this subject, it turns out that lack of time is a bigger stress. The lack of time often causes poor money management, an inability to say no to distractions, and the failure to use one's talents the correct way. But achieving financial freedom leads directly to time freedom. It gives you the ability to say no to work that isn't worth the time or money because you no longer make decisions based on fear. The world opens up when you combine financial and time freedom. It's like a buffet of the good life delivered right to you. Relationships flourish. Family time increases. Regrets diminish. Life moves along at a great pace. It's what most of us want and deserve.

7. Put all of that together and live the life of your dreams with a legacy you can be proud of.

Help who you want when you want. Go where you want when you want. Work on what you want when you want. Build your legacy, and your family's legacy for generations to come. That's total life freedom. What more could you possibly ask for?

I'll take you back to the moment I knew we were on our way to living the life I just described. It was my Rocky moment. On that car ride to New York when Elizabeth got on board with this plan. During that sunny drive Elizabeth told me she was ready to stop being normal, build our business, pay off our debt, and live a life of freedom.

Are you ready to stop being normal?

In that pivotal moment in *Rocky II*, Adrian told Rocky there was one thing she wanted him to do for her, and it's the same thing I want you to do for me.

Win.

So, I'll end with one final question. It's the question Rocky's manager asked right before he got his fighter ready to win the Heavyweight Championship of the World.

What are you waiting for???

ACKNOWLEDGEMENTS

"What is the hardest part about writing a book?"

I've been asked that question over and over during the past few months. This right here, is the hardest part. The idea of leaving out someone who influenced this book, or missing something that I really wanted to share about someone, frightens me more than writing that I was arrested, dead broke or the vast collection of other mistakes I've made. But I'll go anyway and do my best.

First and foremost, I want to thank my wife Elizabeth. Without you, I don't even want to consider where my life would be. You are my better half. You bring calm to my soul during my most frenetic days. You have showed me a greater perspective to life that I would not have without you. You love unconditionally, master motherhood like a hero, give total support on my crazy dreams, hold my feet to the fire and not enable my dramatics, and become more beautiful every day, inside and out.

I love you with all of my heart.

I want to thank our kids: Dylan, Nolan and Andrew.

Dylan- Being the third born, you don't get to go first often enough. So I wanted you to go first here. You have a love for life that has been obvious since the day you were born. Your smile is contagious, you make everyone around you happier and you brighten up each room you walk into. I know perfectly well what the power of your smile can do. In my roughest days, it was a beaming, playful, four-year-old Dylan crawling into bed with me in the morning that gave me the drive to get up every day. You will never understand how much you being you helped me through such a difficult time in my life. Thank you.

Nolan- I live for your morning hug. Nothing feels better than when you wrap your arms around me and don't let go. Your creativity astounds me on a daily basis. Just this morning, you built a homemade swing onto the fort in the backyard. You have never seen a scrap piece of anything without thinking of a way to use it for a project. I wish I had an ounce of your creativity in my body. If there is one thing you do better than being creative, it's thoughtfulness. Your mom and I are certainly not collectors of 'stuff', but what we will always cherish are your unexpected cards and thoughtful gifts that you surprise us with to make us feel so special. This is not to mention your curiosity, which knows no bounds. Please don't ever lose that.

Andrew- Our lives changed forever the night you were born. I knew the moment I held you that my life was no longer about me. Being the first born, your mom and I made our most mistakes with you. We were learning on the job, so please go easy on us in our old age. But despite our mistakes, you are an absolutely amazing young man. Your love of learning is astounding. You have read more books by age of eleven -without being asked- than I did through college. Maybe later. And your love and appreciation for the outdoors just warms my heart. I know that when we look back on this time, our memories will not have been from sitting in front of a television, but of being outside on hikes, looking for bugs, playing games and having a blast together. It was my job to teach you, but you have taught me, and continue to teach me. You teach me how to be more generous. You teach me how to be more helpful. You teach me every day how to be a better dad.

I want to give a very special thank you to my mother and father, Carleen and Vinny. Every opportunity that I have is because of the sacrifices that you have made. Dad, two phrases that you spoke to me during difficult, pivotal parts of my life helped shape my future. Without those words, this book wouldn't be written, and it wouldn't have been possible to help others struggling through the same situations I was. Lives of people you don't know hopefully will be changed because of it. Mom, thank you for your never ending support of my different paths, dreams and goals in life. You have always been there for me no matter how difficult I was to deal with. No matter the situation, I always knew that I had your love. Thank you for everything that you have done to make my life better.

To my brother Steve: Thank you for being the one to guide me through so many years of my life. For supporting me, challenging me, and teaching me how to be strong. For protecting me when I needed it, and for allowing me to fail when I needed that to. You will always be my big brother.

To my mother-in-law, Pat: Thank you for raising such an incredible daughter.

To my Uncle Richie: For planting the photography seed before I could see it.

Outside of my family, well....I know I'm going to mess this up. That's because there are too many people to name, but I'll try. To David Hancock, Stephanie McLawhorn, Aubrey Kosa and the awesome staff at Morgan James Publishing for trusting a unknown author with the chance of a lifetime.

Thank you, Ken Carfagno. You were with me, week after week, as this idea went from nothing to something. For masterminding and brainstorming with me to help me make this book what it is. Thank you, buddy, for being such a great friend.

To Aaron Walker- Without you, this book might still be just a document on my laptop.

To Kyle Shultz- for not only being a great friend, but also for teaming up with me and helping provide a great ending for the book.

To John Briggs, for doing such a marvelous job editing this book.

To my awesome friends David Burke, Larry Hagner, Rob Tannenbaum, Seshu Badrinath, John VanDerMulen, Jamie Slingerland, Stephanie Wharton, and many more, who allowed me to ramble on about stories for the book and for providing valuable feedback.

To all of the podcasters who helped get the word out before this was an actual book- Larry Hagner, Michael O'Neal, Jeremy Slate, Tuan Nguyen, Jaime Jay, Andy Storch, Rick Coplin, Ozeal DeBastos, Joel Kessel, Scott Mulvaney, Christopher and Stephen Duffley Sr., Danny Bauer, Joel Boggess, Raymond Hatfield, Josh Solar, Dave Ballentine, Matt Peet, Matt Holmes, Seshu Badrinath, Matt Inglot, Bryan Argott, Jeff Bouwman and Ray Matz Jr.

To those in the photography and media world who have had a huge influence on my career, this book and on my future One Shot book- J. Bruce Baumann, Marcy Nighswander, Larry Nighswander, Terry Eiler, Tim Ethridge, Bruce Bennett, Brian Winkler, Brian Franey, Justin Rumbach, Dave Lucas, Denny Simmons, Tony DeFazio, Tom Buchanan, Lisa Cunningham, Michael "Z Man" Zagaris, Annie O'Neill, Bob Luckey, John Giamundo, Ryan Scarpino, Jim Dooley, Jeff Schrier, Jim Jorden, Kim Chapin, Matt Campbell, Gavin Smith, Dave Lyons, Jonathan Elmer, Danny Gawlowski, Mike Kopec, Mark Levine, Matt Kryger, Jared Wickerham, Chuck Bennett and many, many more. There are so many more people who should be here. To all of you, I hope you know the impact that you have had. Thank you.

To all of our clients from Elizabeth Vincent Photography- thank you for trusting us with your memories. Your faith in us supported this journey.

To all of my mastermind members for trusting in me, inspiring all of us and making me so proud.

To all of the authors whose books inspired and influenced this book- Seth Godin, Dave Ramsey, Dan Miller, Pat Flynn, Andy Andrews, Zig Ziglar, Shawn Stevenson, Ken Blanchard, Malcolm Gladwell, Napoleon Hill, Tim Ferriss, David J. Schwartz, Robert D. Smith, Jon G. Miller, Robert Kiyosaki, Greg McKeown, Meg Meeker, Jay Conrad Levinson, Simon Sinek, Brendon Burchard, James Altucher, Chris Gilllebeau, John Ruhlin, Rabbi Daniel Lapin, John Taylor Gatto, Dr. Thomas Stanley, William Danko, Og Mandino, Steven Pressfield, Tony Robbins, Brian Moran, Dale Carnegie, Michael Hyatt, Jon Gordon, Richard Branson, Jon Acuff, Rory Vaden, Earl Nightingale, Kevin Leman, Kent Julian, Donald Miller, Charles Duhigg, Ken Coleman, Stephen Covey, Darren Hardy, John Maxwell, Harvey Mackay, and many, many more. This list can go on and on. Thank you for sharing wisdom and knowledge that has helped me in ways that none of you will ever understand. I strive to become that person for someone else.

THE FREEDOM 100

The generous, thoughtful and helpful 100 people who volunteered to read the Freelance to Freedom manuscript and provided feedback, invaluable advice and reviews. Thank you all.

Ryan Olsen	Micheal Jones	Stephen Duffley Sr.
Rachel Theiroff	Thomas Minydzak	Anita Petts
John Lee Dumas	Sarah Gannaway	Ria Fruscello
Deb Belluomini	Steve Roy	David Kincade
Brian Moran	Bill Brent	James Lester
David Cook	Pete Honsberger	Damon Burke
Aaron Walker	Matt Mundt	Ken Hoops
Jeff Pelizzaro	Fereh Ozbek	Ed Betz
Larry Hagner	Lauren Piekos	Rick Coplin
Derek Champagne	Rob Azzalina	Vivian Nania
Carey Green	Neil Young	Andrew Buckwalter
Kyle Lougnot	Shawn Stevenson	Seshu Badrinath
Ernie Lansford	Sarah Leider	Rob Tannenbaum
Matt Miller	Penny Sablosky	John VanDerMeulen
Stephanie Wharton	Deb Ingino	Bryan Argott
Dan Speicher	Dan Miller	John Craig
Kary Oberbrunner	Dustin Belvin	David Burke
John Zugelder	Jerry Schotz	Kelly McNelis
Rob Ainbinder	Beth Underwood	Michael McGreevy
Andy Storch	Miles Revis	Chris Niemeyer
Robert Longley	Fred Marshall	Leeann Marie Golish
Ken Carfagno	Jon Miller	Mark Coomer
Julie Elffers	Sam Lynch	Joe Rogate
Dan Luigs	Jaime Leigh	Anne Stevenson
Adam McCarty	Thomas Recher	Jeff Jochum
Beto Cespedes	Lance Salazar	John Polosky
John Waire	Ozeal DeBastos	Mary Valloni
Seth Godin	Sean Hansen	Jonathan Bates
Darren Everett	Holly Scherer	Raul Figueroa
John Ruhlin	Ashton Palmer	Reggie Shah
Jesse Cleaver	Joel Kessel	Eve Spano Papa
Lena Skully	Greg Lee	Kathy & Al Baca
Donna Lemmer	Brian Seim	
Kent Julian	Michal Stawicki	

BONUS MATERIAL

When writing a book, there is never enough space for everything to make it into the physical book. Thanks to the internet, we can fill those gaps! So if you are enjoying this, and want more behind the scenes stories, please visit

thefreelancetribe.com/bonus

It features bonus stories that didn't make the book, including...

- The story behind what pushed me to started writing Freelance to Freedom.
- The career changing story from Lambeau Field in Green Bay about how I got my first NFL press pass.
- How the mafia got me into a baseball game when I was 15, and what it taught me about life.
- The full story about when I was arrested for stealing (mentioned briefly on page 10).
- What happened when I snuck into Giants Stadium and hid inside of a bathroom stall for four hours just to photograph an NFL game.

Come on over to thefreelancetribe.com/bonus to read these and more!

Also, I run a free online community as well as an exclusive membership site. We support, help and coach ambitious freelancers and small business owners to knock out debt, become financially free, and optimize their businesses to give themselves and their families a life of time, money and location freedom! Please join us!

thefreelancetribe.com

Photo by David Burke

Vincent Pugliese is, first and foremost, a husband to his wife Elizabeth and a father to their three sons, Andrew, Nolan and Dylan.

Vincent has been a professional photojournalist for more than twenty-three years, having been assigned to photograph four United States Presidents, nearly every major sporting event, including multiple Super Bowls, the World Series, the NHL Final, The NCAA Final Four and everything in between. Vincent's work has been published in most major newspapers, magazines and online publications throughout the world.

Vincent, who now coaches and leads small business owners and freelancers towards a life of time, money and work freedom, lives with his family in Pittsburgh, Pennsylvania.

To connect with Vincent, visit www.vincentpugliese.com.

Morgan James Speakers Group

We connect Morgan James published authors with live and online events and audiences who will benefit from their expertise.

Morgan James makes all of our titles available
through the Library for All Charity Organization.

www.LibraryForAll.org